heart
Mind & Soul

Carol,
To a woman with a loving heart, strong mind and caring soul!

Linda Harris :)

With All My Heart, Mind & Soul

A WOMAN'S JOURNEY

LINDA HARRIS

TATE PUBLISHING
AND ENTERPRISES, LLC

With All My Heart, Mind & Soul
Copyright © 2016 by Linda Harris. All rights reserved.

No part of this publication may be reproduced, stored in a retrieval system or transmitted in any way by any means, electronic, mechanical, photocopy, recording or otherwise without the prior permission of the author except as provided by USA copyright law.

The opinions expressed by the author are not necessarily those of Tate Publishing, LLC.

Published by Tate Publishing & Enterprises, LLC
127 E. Trade Center Terrace | Mustang, Oklahoma 73064 USA
1.888.361.9473 | www.tatepublishing.com

Tate Publishing is committed to excellence in the publishing industry. The company reflects the philosophy established by the founders, based on Psalm 68:11,
"The Lord gave the word and great was the company of those who published it."

Book design copyright © 2016 by Tate Publishing, LLC. All rights reserved.
Cover design by Joshua Rafols
Interior design by Richell Balansag

Published in the United States of America

ISBN: 978-1-68270-988-7
1. Body, Mind and Spirit / Inspiration and Personal Growth
2. Religion / Devotional
16.01.20

From My Heart to Yours

A Woman's Journey
This book is not meant to be read in one sitting.
It is devotional in nature and best taken in little bites.
The pages reflect the ponderings of my
mind and soul over two decades.
They came forth from my heart in little bursts
during sporadic times of emotional and spiritual turmoil,
through the ebb and flow of varied relationships,
love and divorce, grief and new understandings.
Thus, from my heart to yours . . .

It is my prayer that God's Spirit
will touch you in some small way through these words.

"The grace of our Lord Jesus Christ be with you.
My love be with you all in Christ Jesus. Amen."
1 Corinthians 16:23-24

A Garden of Rest

In the beginning, in the Garden of Timeless Unity,
Man and woman existed, unaware of their differences,
One with their Maker, without boundaries or a reference of
time. "Today" was forever. All was at rest, no conflict or pain.

Then entered the snake and the eating of forbidden fruit.
Everything shifted, new thoughts exploded in the minds of man.
A knowledge of opposites, time keeping and a sense of self. No
more One, only us and them and a feeling of deep shame.

The Great I Am became obscure as man himself said, "I am."
Blissful intimacy with God became a deep thirst for lust,
Man's desire became an insatiable hunger crouched in fear,
Discontent and loneliness set in, time began its endless reign.

Yet, all was not lost, for the seeds of the fruit held something
fine. Something previously not needed, now decidedly vital.
In the hearts of man, Hope was planted with a measure of Faith.
Promise was given of One who would come and the Garden
reclaim.

An innocent babe, clothed in constraints of time and human form
Would enter the realm of banishment in an act of selfless love,
Bringing with Him the restoration of unity with God,
Enhanced by man's awareness of what he's lost but can regain.

So now beginning has no end for those who accept the gift
Of Grace and Love freely given to vanquish all time and death,
Imbued with Spirit, man's soul is open to the heart of God, A
garden of rest recreated, forever in Jesus' name.

—Linda

Planted in God's Garden

The garden is the perfect analogy for a woman's spiritual journey. Throughout her lifetime a woman will experience times of refreshment, new spiritual awakenings, steady growth and periods of dryness and drought. There will also be times of weeding and discarding, fertilizing and nurturing. I know that I can only guess at your experiences, but I can share with you mine, hoping, that perhaps my story will be a blessing to someone.

From my seedling beginnings, I was always aware of the religious world. I came forth from parents who were dedicating their lives to a particular church and its beliefs. My father was a church school teacher and principal and because of that, this young sprout found herself living in a fishbowl existence. My behavior was scrutinized at every turn and I was often reminded how important it was to be a good example to others. I can still recall the ever present sense that how I acted would reflect on my dad and could affect his job. On the outside, I had turned into one of the artificial plastic plants that the goldfish hide behind in their bowls.

However, I know that inside of me was tender and unsure. And full of questions. I remember many heated discussions around the table at home about the importance of standards and behavior. I was always pushing and prodding for some kind of verbalization that there was really something more important in life. And always, I felt a sense of fear and insecurity, knowing that I was not measuring up to the expectations, at least on the inside. Unknowingly, this attitude was being transferred to how I viewed my relationship with God.

I stayed the course. I tried hard to be a "good girl." I attended church schools and kept myself from too much exposure to the world. It was an "us" and "them" existence. It was like I was a plant being raised in a greenhouse, protected from the worldly elements, safe among my own kind. The church I belonged to was the greenhouse and if I just stayed within it, I would avoid the contamination of pesticides and weed seeds.

I married and continued the family tradition of dedicating my life to working for the church of my youth. I became a teacher myself. I was a sturdy plant on my own. It was during this stage of my life that I felt a deep desire to please God. I felt more than ever the sense of urgency to get my life in order because I could see through the window of the greenhouse that the world was getting to be a crazy place. If I wasn't strong enough when it one day, as predicted, came crashing into my place of refuge, I would succumb and fall to its influence or be crushed into oblivion.

I found myself involved with a group of people who held extreme views about getting one's life in order for the fast approaching end of the world. In my heart, I so much wanted God's favor and I had a great desire to be perfect before Him. I wanted my life purged from all sin and felt it MY duty to make sure I had eradicated all defects from my character. My immersion into fanaticism came from a sincere heart, but sincerity does not automatically result in right.

Thank goodness for the crack in the greenhouse that allowed God's light of truth to shine on me! It was a slow realization that led me to see that I had been deceived. Error had been insidiously cloaked in beautifully sounding familiar words. My initial reaction to discovering that what I was involved in was error, was to shield myself from any falling rain or nourishment. I became dry and brittle inside, while still going through the "good girl" motions on the outside.

It was at this time that my husband and I decided to step out of the greenhouse and become "missionaries" to the world. Despite the fact that we had let ourselves be pulled into fanaticism, we still felt that we had "truth" to offer, at least to poor, ignorant people on the other side of the world.

Living and working in another culture far from the safe walls of my youth, was a turning point for me. It was this experience that opened my eyes to the fact that there were wonderful Christian people outside of my greenhouse existence. They were my friends and they inspired me and demonstrated unconditional love to my family. They were not afraid to talk about Christ and what He had done for them. They were eager to learn and explore more about

God. Their influence helped me to open myself to the rain of God's Spirit on my heart.

Up until this time, my relationship with God had only involved "religion". I had been raised with a list of doctrines that I was to believe in. These doctrines were like little pebbles trying to support my shallow roots. I realized that I did not have a **core** belief. Stepping out into the world had given me a glimpse of the possibilities of a "spiritual" relationship with God. A meaningful, heartfelt one that had nothing whatsoever to do with my behavior. I was slowly awakening to my need for a firm foundation, a single, solid Rock that would hold me tight under any circumstance.

To make a long story short, it has been over the last two decades that the "Linda plant" has slowly turned her petaled head to feel and receive the wondrous love of the SON. I have plowed through all the terminology and behavioral conditioning tapes of my youth to discover ONE simple life-changing truth: God, in the form of Jesus gave HIMSELF to be the debt- payer for ALL the sins of the world, past, present and future! He has fulfilled all the requirements of the law through His death and resurrection. And because of what He did, I AM SAVED! Present tense. Not because of anything I have or could do, but solely because of what He has done.

The ramifications of this truth are that I can say with all certainty, "I have the full assurance of my salvation!" I don't have to fear for the future. I can live with joy now because

I don't just have the longing and hope for salvation. It is a done deal.

This truth makes me feel in awe of my Savior and I want to fall down before Him with adoration and praise for this Wonderful gift of Grace. This truth is both simpler and bigger than any list of requirements and rules of behavior. As a result, I am now freed from the desire to measure and judge others. It is nothing about me and everything about God.

This should be the happily ever after end of my story, but it isn't. Each and every day, I am bombarded with whispers in my ear, old recorded messages, that this simple kernel of truth that I have discovered is "too good to be true." Satan plays with my head with words like, "It can't be that simple." "You should be doing more!"

And sometimes when I share my joy with other plants in the greenhouse of my youth, for some reason it makes them afraid. Their first impulse is to pull out a list of requirements and point out all the things that I must make sure I'm doing. And I have to admit that when the list of requirements is held up next to me, I begin to doubt myself. I just don't measure up. My eyes turn from my Savior in those moments and I begin to lose sight of His wonderful gift to me.

I have come to believe that the only "work" I must do is to daily feed my soul with the truth of the gospel of Jesus Christ. I do this by keeping scriptures before me. The writings of Paul feed my soul and are a constant reminder of the simple truth of God's Grace. One of my favorites scriptural passages however, can be found in Ezekiel 16. These verses present a wonderful word picture of redemption. They bring me comfort when I'm feeling lonely or misunderstood and when I need to be reminded of the wonderful truth that is too good to be true. They tell the story of an abandoned, discarded baby . . .

> "As for your nativity . . .
> **On the day you were born, your cord was not cut, nor were you washed with water to make you clean, nor were you rubbed with salt or wrapped in cloths.**
> **No one looked on you with pity or had compassion enough to do any of these things for you.**
> **Rather you were thrown out into the open field, for on the day you were born, You were despised." Verse 4**

When I read those words, I want to cry. I remember the day my youngest daughter was born. She was born in a primitive hospital on an island in the Pacific. The doctor just hastily wiped her off and handed her to me. It was left up to me to wrap her in a blanket and take her home. I remember the desire I had to quickly give her a warm, cleansing bath and make her squeaky clean.

And that is just what God did when He found this little thrown away infant. Verse 6 . . .

"Then I passed by and saw you kicking about in your blood

> And as you lay there in your blood I said to you, "Live!"
> Then I washed you in water, yes,
> I thoroughly washed off your blood
> And I anointed you with oil.
> I made you thrive like a plant in the field; and you
> grew, matured and became beautiful . . . "

The verses continue the story by telling how God covered this child's nakedness with His wings and entered into a covenant with her. "**And you became Mine!**"

> "I clothed you in embroidered cloth
> and gave you sandals of badger skin;
> I clothed you with fine linen and covered you with silk.
> I adorned you with ornaments, put bracelets on your wrists
> and a chain on your neck.
> And I put a jewel in your nose, earrings in your ears and a
> beautiful crown on your head.
> Thus you were adorned with gold and silver
> and your clothing was of fine linen, silk
> And embroidered cloth. You ate pastry of fine flour,
> honey and oil."

"**You were exceedingly beautiful and succeeded to royalty!**"

Wow! With no effort on her part, with no credentials or illustrious pedigree, this child was adopted into the royal family of God! The clincher for me is verse 14:

> "Your fame went out among the nations because
> of your beauty,
> For it was perfect,
> Through MY splendor which I had bestowed on
> you!"

What a wonderful reminder to us that it is ALL about Jesus and nothing about us! God bestows HIS splendor on us and declares our beauty to be perfect. How awesome is that?

There's even more to this story. You'll read it in the rest of the chapter. Even after this royal treatment by God, this child grows up to reject everything about God. And yet . . . there is such hope and abundant Grace. Look at verses 60-63:

> "Nevertheless, I will remember My covenant with
> you in the days of your youth.
> I will establish an everlasting covenant with
> you . . .
>
> . . . and you will know that I am Lord.
>
> Then when I make atonement for you,
> for all you have done,
> You shall remember and be ashamed and never
> open your mouth anymore because of your shame.
> When I provide you an atonement for all you have
> done, says the Lord God.

What wonderful good news! God's atonement was completed in giving Himself on the cross.

> "We are saved by grace alone, received through faith
> alone, because of the work of Christ alone
> As revealed in the only infallible teacher of truth,
> the Word of God alone!"
>
> —(Desmond Ford)

That is the gospel. It is my prayer that you will believe and hold this wonderful truth close to your own heart. May you be

"like a tree planted by the rivers of water, that brings forth fruit in its season, whose leaf also shall not wither." Ps. 1:3

Dancing in the Arms of God

"Come dance with
Me," He said.
Large strong hands reached
out to me. There was
longing in their stretch.

Our fingers touched,
"Please take My hand,
Let Me heal your
hurting soul."
My heart cried, "Yes!"
That was all it took.
He held on and
pulled me close.

"Allow Me," were the
only words He spoke,
As we moved across the floor,
dancing palm in palm
and cheek to cheek, my
arms around His side.

It was then I felt
the scars and
tears welled in my eyes
As I realized what this
dance had cost.
I pulled back, but
He held me tight
And whispered
softly in my ear,

"The debt's been paid,
my precious one.
It's time to celebrate!
So let the dance go on!

—Linda

"Dancing in the Arms of God" was inspired by a book that painted a picture of God as One who considers us to be the desire of His heart.

Have you ever watched couples ballroom dancing? They look so graceful and beautiful floating across the dance floor. And for some reason, in those moments of coordinated teamwork, the couple appears connected in a special way. They boldly look in each other's eyes and hold each other in an embrace that seems to tell their partner that they are cherished.

I don't know much about dancing, but one evening I went with my parents to a dance and dinner at the Elks Lodge. My mom and dad learned to ballroom dance several years ago. I love to watch them. This particular evening, my father took me out on the dance floor with him. His expertise and confidence in leading gave me the sensation of being a wonderful dancer myself! For a few brief minutes, I had the thrill of being held in someone's arms, dancing as if I had been doing it for years.

Can you picture your Heavenly Father holding you in His arms and leading you around the dance floor? He holds you close, as if He never wants to let you go. You feel beautiful and ever so cherished in His arms. Don't pull back. Let Him hold you and guide you with His loving touch. Listen to what He wants to whisper in your ear. And never let Him go!

Tears In A Bottle

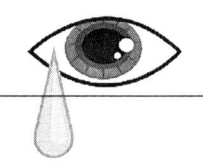

Tears in a bottle,
The soul's salty rain.
Mixture of emotions,
A reminder of pain.

Tears in a bottle,
The essence of grief,
A potion of sorrow,
Heart-rending relief.

Put my tears in Your bottle,
In Your book, are they not?
When I cry out to you,
Do You give me a thought?

Yes, tears in a bottle,
In the palm of Your hand.
Sweet-smelling perfume,
Only You understand.

—Linda

Tears in a Bottle

"You number my wanderings,
Put my tears into Your bottle;
Are they not in Your book?
When I cry out to You,
Then my enemies will turn back;
This I know, because God is for me."
Psalm 56:8

I've cried many tears. Tears of sadness, sorrow, pain and joy. Tears that cleanse and tears that help grieve. These verses tell us that our tears do not go unnoticed by God. In fact, they are recorded forever in His Book of Tears and stored away in a beautiful bottle.

It brings to mind the image of Mary bending over the feet of Jesus, anointing him with her tears and a costly perfume and then wiping the tears and perfume away with her long, flowing hair. Jesus cherished her gift in His heart as He faced the ordeal ahead of Him.

I know that God does not need a reminder of why He came to this earth to die for mankind, but I still like to think that the tears of His dear ones held in a bottle are a reminder to Him of just why He made the ultimate sacrifice. And

I can imagine Him one day taking that precious bottle of tears and pouring the contents out into the empty space of the universe and saying, "It is finished!"

> "And God shall wipe away all tears
> from their eyes, there shall be no more death,
> nor sorrow, nor crying; and there shall be no more pain,
> for the former things have passed away." Revelation
> 21:4

Deep Calls Upon Deep

A thirsty soul, lost in a dry and barren land,
An empty, lonely discontent.
Tears, the only nourishment,
False hopes the only sustenance.

Deep calls upon deep,
A prayer to the God of my life.

A mirage of peace shimmers on the sand,
A beckoning, enticing scent.
Dry, parched dreams, unsatisfied,
Despair upon the countenance.

Deep calls upon deep,
A cry to the God Most High.

A soft shadow cools the weary brow,
A reviving, soothing breeze,
Take comfort, broken heart laid bare,
Sorrow fade away.

Deep calls upon deep,
A prayer to the God of my Strength.

A mighty rock, the refuge now,
A shelter that will ease,
Springing from the ground comes life,
Hope begins this day.

(See Psalms 42)

—Linda

Psalm 42: "Yearning for God in the Midst of Distresses"

**"Why are you cast down, O my soul?
And why are you disquieted within me? Hope in
God, for I shall yet praise Him
for the help of His countenance.
Deep calls upon deep at the noise of
Your waterfalls. All Your waves and billows have
gone over me. The Lord will command
His loving kindness in the daytime,
and in the night His song shall be with me,
A prayer to the God of my life."
Verses 6-8**

One summer I took a slow train to Mazatlan, Mexico. We traveled for two full days and nights through the hot Sonoran desert. The train seemed to stop at every cactus along the way and the biting sand blew in through the open windows, turning our pale skin brown with dust. I did not sleep at all during the trip. In the middle of the second night, I was standing between two train cars. I was feeling miserable and for one brief moment I had the urge to throw myself off the train so that I could lie down in the desert and die! My companions and I laugh about it now, but at the moment it happened, it was a dreadful place to be in my body and mind.

In the film, "Hidalgo", the main character, Frank and his horse are involved in a race across the Saharan desert.

Near the end of the movie, there is a point when the main character and his horse are injured and dying in the middle of the broiling sands. The horse falls and Frank soon follows, sinking to his knees in despair and physical exhaustion. As he lays sprawled in the hot sand, Frank's inner spirit begins to call out to a higher power. He begins to hallucinate and soon sees images of his Indian ancestors, the very ancestors that he had tried to deny as part of himself. When he finally acknowledges his Indian heritage, he gains the strength and will to carry on and finish the race.

I think that both of these experiences illustrate what David is talking about in Psalm 42. It is the experience of almost every woman at some point in her life. It may be a physical crisis, but more likely it will be a crisis of the heart and soul. When it happens, just remember that our inner spiritual soul is programmed to call out to the Creator for sustenance. And as these verses tell us, He **will** answer. Never give up hope!

Doesn't She Know?

She tugs on my arm,
Almost steps on my toes.
Her wide eyes sparkle and
Her brown face glows.

"Teacher, guess what?"
She squeezes me tight.
"I get to pretend
I'm a princess tonight!"

Doesn't she know?
Hasn't somebody told her?

"Teacher, did
you hear me?
I can't hardly wait.
I'll be somebody special.
Won't that be great?"

Doesn't she know?
Hasn't somebody told her?

"Teacher please listen,
My dress is so white,
It will make me so pretty,
Especially tonight!"

Doesn't she know?
Hasn't somebody
told her?

"Oh, Teacher,
here's more!
There's a crown
for my head.
It's fit for a princess,
That's what
my mom said."

Doesn't she know?
Why haven't I told her?
She's the child of the King,
She's His very own daughter.

Linda Harris

He'll clothe her in raiment,
As white as can be.
He'll put jewels in her crown,
It's a gift to her free.
She should know she is special,
God couldn't do less,
Than make her His own and
Call her His princess!

—Linda

The idea for this poem came during the week of Halloween. My students were excited about going trick-or treating and dressing in costumes. One little third grade girl was telling me how she was going to dress up like a princess.

As a teacher in public school, I have to be careful about talking with my students about God. I do my best to give input if they ask me questions. It is amazing how often their minds lead them to ask questions about God, the angels and even the devil. The little ones from Mexico seem especially superstitious and curious about the supernatural realm.

When I start to lose my focus in teaching, I try to remind myself that although I cannot tell the children outright about how much God loves them, I can do my best to let God shine through me. I pray each day that somehow they will get the idea that they are loved by God and me. I want them to have a spiritual hunger that will someday lead them to a relationship with Jesus. They need to know that they are children of the Heavenly Father, members of the royal household.

In the same way, I think that in each woman is a little, insecure girl who still longs to feel as special and cherished as a princess. Perhaps that is why there are so many variations of the Cinderella story that can be found all around the world.

This poem is dedicated to the little girl in each of you. Read it and know that you are His very own daughter, His very own princess!

Song of Faith

Tho the fig tree may not blossom
Nor the fruit be on the vine,
I will make the Lord my strength,
I will joy in the Divine.

Tho the fields yield no good harvest,
Tho the flocks all disappear,
I will make the Lord my strength,
I will have no need to fear.

The Lord God is my strength.
He is my one true Friend.
He will give me feet to climb,
To high places I've never been.
(See Habakkuk 3:17-19)

—Linda

> **Habakkuk 3:17-19: A Hymn of Faith**
>
> **"Though the fig tree may not blossom, nor fruit be on the vines, Though the labor of the olive may fail, and the fields yield no food: Though the flock be cut off from the fold, and there be no herd in the stalls, Yet I will rejoice in the Lord, I will joy in the God of my salvation.**
> **The Lord God is my strength; He will make my feet like the deer's feet.**
> **And He will make me walk on my high hills."**

"Song of Faith" is a paraphrase of the above verses. It was written in response to a Bible study group leader asking each member to try and write a song based on a Bible verse. These verses have given me courage and inspiration to keep hanging on even when things are looking bleak and hopeless.

These verses are also the inspiration behind Hannah Hurnard's book, "Hinds' Feet on High Places." In one part of the story, the main character, Much Afraid, has just journeyed out of the mist and clouds. The Shepherd joins her at one point and tells her:

> **"When you continue your journey there may be more mist and cloud. Perhaps it may even seem as**

though everything you have seen here of the High Places was just a dream, or the work of your own imagination. But you have seen reality and the mist which seems to swallow it up is the illusion. Believe steadfastly in what you have seen. Even if the way up to the High Places appears obscured and you are led to doubt whether you are following the right path, remember the promise, 'Thine ears shall hear a word behind thee, saying, This is the way, walk ye in it, when ye turn to the right hand and when ye turn to the left.' Always go forward along the path of obedience as far as you know it until I intervene, even if it seems to be leading you where you fear I could never mean you to go."

The Little Things

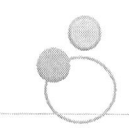

The little things,
They get me down.
Small nothing things
That make me frown.

My life is blessed.
My family's well.
Yet all I want to do is yell!

My job's ok.
The pay is fair.
So why do I feel
Such deep despair?

I roll my eyes
And groan and moan.
My voice takes on
a nasty tone.

I'm always asked,
"Why are you mad?"
It seems as if
I'm never glad.

It does no good
To show much gloom.
Why do I have
Such thoughts of doom?

This attitude is hard to shake.
It's also hard for me to take.

Out of this pit
I need to climb.
It's such a struggle
All the time.

I must look up,
I must hold tight.
I must stand still
And let God fight.

Give God control.
Just let go.
He's the answer
This I know.

—Linda

Today is a good day to write about the little things. I woke up cranky because my allergy medicine kept me awake all night. When I went to put on my only white shirt, I saw that it was stained with ink. I didn't have time to eat breakfast and I spilled the contents of my purse in the car. It was a rainy day and the kids at school had to stay in for recess. The 5th graders in my reading class have decided to stop learning and I raised my voice in irritation (okay, I yelled!) when someone decided to ignore my instructions! It's the little things that get me down!

Do you ever feel like things are getting out of control in your life? You are not alone. 2 Chronicles 20 tells the story of a situation in which a group of people were feeling like things in their life were getting out of hand.

> **"It happened after this that the people of Moab with the people of Ammon and others with them besides the Ammonites, came to battle against Jehosphaphat. Then some came and told Jehosphaphat saying, 'A great multitude is coming against you from beyond the sea!'"**

In other words, "Help!" Things are getting out of control fast! What are we going to do?"

Jehoshaphat gathered all the people together in one place and proclaimed a fast throughout all the land. He then stood before the congregation of all Judah and Jerusalem and prayed to God. He reminded God of His great power and how He had helped His people in the past. That tells me that Jehosphaphat was pretty confident in his relationship with God. He was also willing to admit how powerless he and the people of Judah were and how much they needed God's help. And God answered:

"Do not be afraid nor dismayed because of this great multitude, for the battle is not yours, but God's. You will not need to fight in this battle. Position yourselves, stand still and see the salvation of the Lord, who is with you. Do not fear or be dismayed, tomorrow go out against them, for the Lord is with you."

While the people of Judah were facing a very big thing in this instance, I think the principle of how it was dealt with applies to the challenging little things, too. Big or little, it all boils down to a feeling of losing control. In actuality, losing control may be the best thing to happen to us. It is then that we let God take control.

A Price So Deep

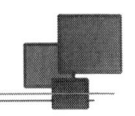

God's love is never sloppy,
His grace is never cheap.
Both fall to earth from heaven
At a cost that runs so deep.

The blood price has been paid.
God's love shone through His Son.
Man's debt to sin is cancelled.
Christ saw that it was done.

Are you feeling worn and weary?
Is your guilty soul laid low?
Look up to see God's grace rain down,
It all around you flows.

God's love and grace are free,
There's no deposit, no return.
There's nothing you can do,
And that's all that you must learn.

Sweet love will heal your wounded heart.
His grace will set you free.
He'll take the burdens from your soul
And happy you will be.

—Linda

"A Price So Deep" was my very emotional response to a comment that was made during a Bible class discussion at church. Our group was talking about faith versus works. A comment was made about God's love being the only important thing in this life in regards to our salvation. A woman responded by saying that love alone was not enough. In fact that was what she termed, "sloppy love" and "cheap grace." I was appalled at those incongruous terms! It saddened me to think that someone might liken God's grace to something that was cheap.

> **"Of how much worse punishment, do you suppose, will he be thought worthy who has trampled the Son of God underfoot, counted the blood of the covenant by which he was sanctified a common thing, and insulted the Spirit of Grace?" Heb. 10:29**

I think that one of Satan's greatest deceptions is to get us to think that somehow we have a part to play in our salvation. We fall into this trap so easily because our lives are a constant game of give and take; hard work and reward. How many times have I told my own children, "if it's too good to be true, it must not be true!" And yet, the atoning sacrifice of Jesus, while so undeserving, IS true! Our most difficult "work" in this life is to accept that truth.

> **"But now the righteousness of God apart from the law is revealed, being witnessed by the Law and the Prophets, even the righteousness of God which is through faith in Jesus Christ to all and on all who believe. For there is no difference; for all have sinned and fall short of the glory of God, being justified freely by His grace through the redemption that is in Christ Jesus." Romans 3:21-24**

God's love is NEVER sloppy. His grace is NEVER cheap! It costs us nothing, yet with blood and the anguish of His soul, God sacrificed everything to ensure that this wonderful gift is available to all. Simply believe!

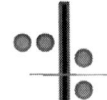

When I Sit In Darkness

Therefore, I will look unto the Lord;
I will wait for the God of my salvation;
My God will hear me.

Rejoice not against me, O mine enemy;
When I fall, I shall arise;
When I sit in darkness,
The Lord shall be a light unto me.

He will bring me forth to the light;
And I shall behold his righteousness.

Micah 7:7-9

There are days God seems so far and away.
My life up close appears void and gray.

Near-sighted vision is bleak and narrow.
Guilt, pain and loneliness bow my head low.

I crawl in a tunnel of self-pity and doubt.
I cower in fear, thinking there's no way out.

As I sit in darkness, a soft breeze blows by.
I lift my head and I look up high.

I stand, step back and peer at the light.
My eyes want to close and keep it from sight.

Gentle words whisper and bid me to see.
"My child, I'm here with you, won't you look upon Me?"

I'm there in the distance, shining with might,
And I'm here in the darkness holding you tight!"

—Linda

As a child, I was very much afraid in the dark. And I have to admit that there are times now, even as a grown woman, that I find that old monster of fear creeping in on me if I am home alone at night. It is interesting how sounds are magnified in the darkness and how the imagination takes over and conjures up amazingly outrageous ideas about what could possibly be slinking around in the night.

I sometimes struggle with a darkness that lurks in the corners of my mind and soul. It comes in the form of worry and melancholy. It's a slow, insidious creature that comes unbidden as negative thoughts and feelings of hopelessness at the conditions in the world around me. And there are even times when I seem to flirt with the darkness when I let depression settle in like an old friend.

In the past, when I have felt the darkness taking a hold of my soul, I have tried to either pretend it wasn't there, because after all, it shouldn't be there, or fight against it with all my might. I have come to see that both of these methods of dealing with depression and darkness do not work. Now, when I sense a time of darkness coming upon me, I *acknowledge* it instead of deny it and then I figure out how to *get through* it rather than battle against it.

There is a wonderful book, titled, "When the Heart Waits", by Sue Monk Kidd. She likens the spiritual journey to that of a butterfly. She brings out the point that a beautiful butterfly can only come from a time of darkness in the cocoon:

"Whenever new life grows and emerges, darkness is crucial to the process. Whether it's the caterpillar in the chrysalis, the seed in the ground, the child in the womb, or the True Self in the soul, there's always a time of waiting in the dark."

It is also her belief that this is what Jesus was referring to when He was talking to Nicodemus about a spiritual birth. She says that Jesus was "implying that with every birth there is a womb, and if we want to find the inner kingdom, we will have to enter the place of waiting, darkness, and incubation." She concludes by saying, "When we enter the spiritual night, we can feel alone, encompassed by a fearful darkness. What we need to remember is that we're carried in God's womb, in God's divine heart, even when we don't know it, even when God seems far away." (page 149)

So take heart. When darkness comes your way, wait with patient anticipation for the light of dawn to come. It will reveal the wonderful results of the workings of the night. And remember, God is right there with you through it all.

The Greatest Gift

LOVE IS
The essence of God,
The sum of the whole.
The beginning and end.
Universe in control.

GOD IS
Love suffering long, Kind, without pride,
Caring, without arrogance,
A refuge to hide.

GOD IS
Love rejoicing in truth,
Crying tears over sin
Bearing all things
Causing hope to begin.

GOD IS
Love never failing,
Enduring all things,
The vine to which faith holds
And tenaciously clings.

LINDA HARRIS

GOD IS
Faith, Hope and Love, Three Beings, one
mind. To Him open your heart,
And love you will find.

LOVE IS
The best gift of all,
We'll see face to face,
When Heaven's gates open
We'll look fully on Grace.

—Linda

"Love is the answer, no matter the question."

I'll have to reveal a little "dirty" secret of mine to acknowledge the author of the above quote. I came across it while reading a book by Mary Balogh, who happens to be a romance novel writer. I hesitate to share the source of the quote above, not because I feel guilty about the fact that I read an occasional romance novel, but rather because I don't want to trivialize such a profound statement.

These simple words succinctly describe the core of my spiritual foundation. Let me put it in context. I grew up submersed in a cultic culture of exclusivity. The church of my "youth" was one in which its members were indoctrinated with the idea that they belonged to the one true church. The idea was and still is, that all other Christians would one day come to see this fact and all who truly loved God would join this last remnant church. My own good and ultimately perfect works plus my own conjured up faith were my only guarantees for entrance into heaven. You can imagine that I never quite measured up. (After all, I read romance novels!!)

Even now, as I stand in a place of God's grace and understand that there is absolutely NOTHING that I can or cannot do that will ensure my salvation, I am sometimes confronted by those who are still caught in the tangle of their own useless attempts at trying to gain their "golden ticket" into heaven. I hear, "Yes, Jesus saves, BUT......." I start to say that there is no BUT, and then get accused of promoting "cheap grace."

How does one explain that finding my rest and liberty in the New Covenant of Jesus has enlarged my sense of responsibility? I don't have a one day of week religion anymore. I put my trust in God each and every day! He is my moment by moment, daily rest. It is ALL about HIM! And because He has ensured my salvation, I am left with a sense of awe that prompts me to center my whole life with His love. In everything I do and say I want to remember the quote above: "Love is the answer, no matter the question!"

Such good intentions I have! Ah ... but when I mess up, and I do much too often ... .I am never in fear that I have somehow, by my failure to love, had my name blotted from the Book of Life. I just have to remind myself that MY failure to love is a given. But because God IS love, HE is always the answer!

The idea that love simply IS ... .has led me to a sort of epiphany that struck me on a recent Valentine's Day. While this holiday is usually associated with mushy love and tangible displays of emotion in the form of chocolate and flowers, I was struck with the idea that God's love has to do with an absence of such emotions.

Now don't get me wrong. I'm all for the warm, fuzzy feeling I get when I read about God's love for me. "For God so loved the world that He gave His only begotten Son . . ." My moment of clarity has to do with the fact that God's love toward mankind has nothing whatsoever to do with emotion. And it is this fact that makes it the best love of all. Simply stated:

God IS, ……therefore, Love IS!

"Look up into the sky and see the clouds high above you.
If you sin, what do you accomplish against Him?
Even if you sin again and again, what effect will it have on Him?
If you are good, is this some great gift to Him?
What could you possibly give Him?
No, your sins affect only people like yourself, and Your good deeds affect only other people."
Job 35:5-8

God IS……therefore, Love IS!

Nothing I do FOR God or AGAINST Him affects His love towards me! Wow! God's love exists despite me. I can rail against Him, curse Him, pound my fists against His chest and He will stand there calmly loving me. I can do mighty things for Him, live a life of service and sacrifice and He will stand there calmly loving me. God is not about emotion. He just IS!

This kind of love is very foreign to us humans. We live out our lives always searching for something to satisfy the deep hunger and need for love in our hearts. Sometimes that means we overmedicate or go from one bad relationship to another. Sometimes we do find a satisfying earthly love, but invariably we continue to hunger and thirst for something that always seems to be just out of reach.

I am thinking that perhaps it would help if we could understand the truth of God's love just being something that simply exists with no strings attached. If there is nothing at all that I can do that will affect God's love for me, that gives me a huge sense of relief! I don't have to always be thinking that I might have some unconfessed sin that might separate me from Him or be thinking that I SHOULD be doing something more for Him in order to be loved by Him. One of my worse fears has been that I might somehow disappoint God. But if God's love simply IS–then there is nothing that I can do that will disappoint Him!

There is peace and rest in the knowledge that God's love is not emotional. It doesn't change under any circumstance.

It is not fickle or varying in degree. It simply IS! Perhaps this truth taken into our hearts will ease our manic attempts to feel the emotions of human love. Enjoy the hearts and flowers. Enjoy those moments of passion and lovemaking. But rest in the knowledge that with or without those things, YOU ARE LOVED simply and always and that NOTHING you do or don't do will change that truth!

Short Circuit

They lie close together,
But they're both so alone.
Their limbs intertwine,
But they've hearts cold as stone.

The silence hangs heavy,
Each longs to speak out,
Fear shuts the door,
There's room only for doubt.

Bodies are touching,
But no connection is made.
They lie there and wonder,
When did the spark fade?

A lifetime of hurts
And misunderstanding,
Searching for love,
But not really finding.

Along separate paths,
How long can they travel,
Till whatever is left
Comes completely unraveled?

—Linda

Loneliness
*"My heart is stricken and withered like grass . . . .
I lie awake, and am like a sparrow alone on the housetop."*
Psalm 102:4,7

If there ever was a formula for loneliness, I would say that it would be this:

Disconnection x Close Physical Proximity = Degree of Loneliness

In other words, the closer you are to a person in a physical sense and the more you feel disconnected in any way to them, the greater will be your sense of loneliness. Feeling alone in a crowd is one thing. Feeling alone in a marriage is something altogether more intense and painful. Being separated from loved ones through time, distance or death brings its share of painful loneliness, but I would venture to say that it is within a marriage relationship that a woman can feel the most alone.

Happy ending expectations set us up for dissatisfaction and disappointment. We cling to the dream that we will find our soul mate and live happily ever after with our best friend. There are some who do find such true love. But I would venture to guess that many others only find disillusionment. We desire total acceptance and understanding from our spouse, but so many times we feel misunderstood and criticized. Whatever the reason, our marriage invariably falls short of our expectations. When that happens, we refocus and adjust and go on the best we can. But deep inside, we struggle with feeling alone and we wonder if there is anyone out there who can ever see into our heart and soul and truly understand who we are.

Looking to another human for this kind of understanding will always yield disappointment. That is why we must look only to God. He is our soul mate. Only He can ease our loneliness and fill us with satisfying love.

"For your Maker is your husband, the
Lord of hosts is His name.
And your Redeemer is the Holy One of Israel:
He is called the God of the whole earth,
For the Lord has called you,
Like a woman forsaken and grieved in spirit,
Like a youthful wife when you were refused, Says your God.
For a mere moment I have forsaken you,
But with great mercies I will gather you . . .
With everlasting kindness I will have mercy
on you, says the Lord, your Redeemer."
Isaiah 54:5-8

The Face in the Mirror

The face in the mirror
Won't look me
straight in the eye.
She looks away from my gaze
Without telling me why.

Imprisoned and lonely
Between silver and glass,
She's locked in a cold place,
Emotional impasse.

Her lips form my name
But no sound can I hear.
The image gets fuzzy,
It's no longer clear.

Remote, disconnected,
Drifting away.
Where are you going?
Why won't you stay?

—Linda

Reflection

When we first discover mirrors as little girls, we want to look at our reflection in them all the time. We dance and strut and grin at ourselves with delight. As we get older and discover boys, we spend many hours in front of the mirror making sure that we look just right.

Then come the years of having no time at all to look in the mirror, we are so busy with husband, kids, home and work. We pride ourselves on being able to get ready for our day with only five minutes in front of the bathroom mirror. And if we were really honest, we would admit that we are happy not to reflect much on our slowly expanding midriffs, the specks of gray in our hair and the wrinkles around our eyes. And in time, we learn to get by with not looking at ourselves at all! When was the last time that you really looked deep into your own eyes? Can you even do it now? Who do you see? The trouble is that women tend to evolve into creations of other people's expectations. We become conforming, pliant blobs of clay that we let other people punch, twist, pull and form into images of what they want us to be. Somewhere along the way, we lose the unique essence of who God made us to be. We become invisible to ourselves.

The good news is that while we may have lost a sense of ourselves, God has never lost us! The entire book of the Psalms reflects the soul's cry to be found by God and the constant reassurance that God has never forgotten the one who feels lost.

> **"In my distress I called upon the Lord, and cried out to my God;**
> **He heard my voice from His temple, and my cry came before Him, even to His ears." Psalm 18:6**

God doesn't just see us from the outside. He sees us from the inside out. We are His temple. We carry Him with us in Spirit, which means that He is always seeing, hearing and knowing us from the depths of our soul. It is comforting to know that in those times that we cannot see ourselves clearly, God sees us crystal clear. And loves us just the way we are! The next time you look at yourself in the mirror, look with confidence that whoever is staring back at you is someone who is near and dear to the heart of God. Perhaps that will give you the courage to discover yourself again.

A Tribute

Her stay on earth flashed
Briefly in the twinkling eye of time.

Silent, dark destruction tore away the shell
And the breath of life returned to God.

But her spirit of love remained earthbound
And with the extinguishing of the light.
Her soul released the sweet perfume of Grace.

It traveled on the wind.
Enveloped in the midst of Hope.

The fragrance of a spirit-filled life fell upon hearts
Torn open wide and wet with grief.

And slowly with degrees of time.
The essence of her joyful days became a balm to
Soothe and mend and water seeds of love.

So while her time on earth was brief, Her body was the vessel.

To carry unbroken, a golden chain.
The message of God's Amazing Grace.

Left behind, we long for just one more touch.
In looking deep, we find it in our hearts
In the stirrings of kindness, hope and love.

—Linda

It was at a women's ministry retreat that Bev first shared her worry about her health. Even though she was physically very active, she exercised daily, went hiking on a regular basis with her family of four boys, and ate as healthily as possible, she was feeling tired and worn down. She told us that she would be going in to the doctor's the week after our weekend get-away and asked for our prayers to ease her concerns.

There were 13 of us at that retreat. A mishmash of personalities. Some of us strangers and some casual acquaintances, while others like Bev, came with their best friend. It was a wonderful weekend of spiritual blessing and bonding. Anxiety, fears, joys and concerns were shared. Shyness was overcome and fun was had by all. It was an unforgettable experience with sisters in Christ. It was also the last retreat that Bev would ever attend. We buried her seven months later.

As I sat in the church at her memorial, I cried for a beautiful life cut short. She died days short of her 50th birthday. But I also felt such peace in that place of tribute to her. She had lived her life with beauty and grace. I could imagine her soul lifting off to heaven leaving a ripple of love behind her, touching so many lives, even in her death.

It made me reflect on my own life on this earth. What will I leave in my wake? It is a worthy question for each of us to ask ourselves. Will I be a part of that unbroken chain representing God's Grace?

> **"But God, who is rich in mercy, because of His great love with which He loved us, even when we were dead in trespasses, made us alive together with Christ (by grace you have been saved), and raised us up together, and made us sit together in the heavenly places in Christ Jesus, that in the ages to come He might show the exceeding riches of His grace in His kindness toward us in Christ Jesus." Ephesians 2:4-5**

The Soul

A place entombed in flesh,
Yet transcending any barriers
To soar to reaches far and wide.

A lonely place
Conflicted, torn surreal.

Untouched by hands
Yet breached with words,
A strange land of reality.

The sight behind closed eyes,
Painting images in the dark,
To see, down deep inside the heart.

A safe place
For probing hopes and doubts,
Where silent tears, quiet laughter,
Tender longings find a refuge.

—Linda

> **Soul**: Hebrew: nephesh: vitality, a breathing creature Greek: psucho: to gently breathe, spirit, heart

"What does the Lord your God require of you, but to fear the Lord your God, to walk in all His ways and to love Him, to serve the Lord your God with all your heart and with all your *soul*." Deut. 10:12

"You have lovingly delivered my **soul** from
the pit of corruption,
You have cast all my sins behind Your back."
Isaiah 38:17

"The Lord redeems the *soul* of His servants and none of those who trust in Him shall be condemned." Psalm 34:22

"And my **soul** shall be joyful in the Lord;
It shall rejoice in His salvation.
All my bones shall say, Lord, who is like you?"
Psalm 35:9

**"Lord, God of my salvation, I have cried out day and night before You.
Let my prayer come before You; Incline Your ear to my cry.**

For my *soul* is full of troubles." Psalm 88:1
For the word of God is living and powerful, and sharper than any two-edged sword,
piercing even to the division of **soul** and spirit, and of joints and marrow,
and is a discerner of the thoughts and intents of the heart." Heb. 4:12

Heaviness

**"The problem isn't time,
the problem is heaviness."**
Theophane the Monk, Tales of a
Magic Monastery

Some days I'm full of energy and flying high. I feel confident and able to accomplish anything. Then imperceptibly, little drops of doubt and fear begin to patter down on my wings. I don't notice them at first. Then I feel a tug and a pull at my heart. I hear, "Who do you think you are?"

The sprinkles become a downpour and before I know it I'm grounded. With a thunk! My energy is drained and I am weary. My soul feels heavy. I feel alone. I stop moving and I wonder, "What's the point?" I start to drown in a sea of self-incrimination and pity.

Can you relate?

What is the heaviness in your life? Sometimes it is simply anxiety over the unknown, or fear over change. Unfulfilled expectations, misunderstandings or a sense of not feeling good enough can create weighty burdens on our hearts.

At this time in my own life, it is a reoccurring sense that because I have a failed marriage and find myself alone, that I am unlovable. My intellect tells me that is a silly notion. I have wonderful friends and a supportive family. Reality tells me that I was lonely and unhappy in my dysfunctional marriage. And yet, I sometimes stand in the rain of doubt and self-pity and let myself get waterlogged with fear.

I recently read an excerpt from one of Melody Beattie's devotionals. She says,

> **"In reality, we're too worried, obsessed, doubtful, overly concerned, and afraid. Release all that heaviness in your mind and heart. Let it sink away so you can stand free from its weight. When all the heaviness drops away, you can float through and above your ordinary life. You'll decide how you want to live rather than letting circumstances of the day control you."** (More Language of Letting Go, pg. 350)

How can we let go? It sometimes takes mental energy to let go of these negative thoughts and rise above the clouds. When I find myself standing in the dark, rainy clouds of negative thoughts, I have learned to take these steps:

1. Acknowledge what I am thinking and feeling.
2. Think to identify the source of fear that it comes from. Many times this means pinpointing the lie that someone planted in your head.

3. Surrender the lie, or negative, obsessive thought.
4. Ask God to replace it with a truth.
5. Focus on the truth and repeat it out loud if necessary until it becomes stuck in your head!
6. Repeat as needed!

Remember these famous words?

> **"Come to me, all of you who are weary and carry heavy burdens, and I will give you rest... . .**
> **You WILL find rest for your souls."** Matthew 11:28

He Says, She Says

He says, She says,
But neither can agree.

"It didn't happen!"
"Yes, It did!"
Distorted Reality.

How can two people
Be so different,
Their minds so far apart?
They fail to see down
deep inside
Each other's bleeding heart?

"I'm right! You're wrong!
It's crystal clear to me."

"You never listen."
They both repeat.
How is it they can't see?

Is there any hope
For these two souls?
Between them stands a wall.
It's too far up,
Too far around,
The barrier stands so tall!

—Linda

Is There Any Hope?

Many of us feel the most disheartened when we find ourselves in the midst of a broken relationship. The conflict and misunderstanding send daggers into our heart. The wounds are made much more painful with the thrusts of rash words that cut and slice away at our ego and spirit. It is when we stand surrounded by the carnage of such an emotional battle, that we feel the most hopeless. Can this relationship be mended? How can we pick up the pieces of our obliterated hearts and reestablish a connection with our friend, child or spouse?

The book of Lamentations is a portrayal of a devastatingly broken relationship between God and His people. The Israelites divorced themselves from God and it wasn't too long before they found themselves in bondage in a place far from home. In Chapter 3, the prophet of Lamentations is recounting the pain and anguish that has resulted from a separation from God.

> "You have moved my soul far from peace; I have forgotten prosperity.
> And I said, "My strength and my hope have perished from the Lord." Verse 18

But even in the middle of his crying and despair, the prophet catches sight of a bit of hope and hangs on with all his might. He realizes that despite all that has happened to bring about a seemingly irreconcilable relationship, there is hope!

> "This I recall to my mind, therefore I have hope.
> Through the Lord's mercies we are not consumed, because His compassions fail not.
> They are new every morning; Great is Your faithfulness.
> The Lord is my portion, says my soul. Therefore I hope in Him!
> The Lord is good to those who wait for Him,
> |to the soul who seeks Him.
> It is good that one should hope and wait quietly for the salvation of the Lord." Vs. 21-27

> Take heart! God can mend any broken relationship. "I will go before you and make the crooked places straight." (Isa. 45:2) Never give up hope. Hang onto it with all your might.

The One Who Stayed Home

The one who stayed home was a faithful son.
He did his duty till each job was done.
He was a worthy example, a dependable man.
He stayed to the task and followed the plan.

The one who stayed home, worked hard every day.
From dawn until dusk, without any pay.
The firstborn son never whined or complained. He
was admired by all and steadfast remained.

But the one who stayed home hid a dark secret within.
A deep, frozen anger in his heart had set in.
Obedience and duty became a burden so great.
Resentment grew strong, distrust bordered on hate.

The one who stayed home became a man lost,
In his own house a stranger, unaware of the cost.
The price was the absence of joy in his heart,
The failure to see His Father's love from the start.

When the one who had strayed fell down on his knees,
The one who stayed home turned his back on the pleas.

He turned a deaf ear to his Father's voice . . .
"My son has returned. Come let us rejoice!"

He watched as his Father opened loving arms wide,
To encompass the prodigal AND the one lost inside.
To the one who stayed home,
The Father spoke words that were true,
"You're with Me always,
All I have is for you!"

"I love all My children. Each of you I embrace.
Please give Me your heart to fill with My grace!"

—Linda

The One Who Stayed Home was inspired by Henri J.M. Nouwen's book, "The Return of the Prodigal Son." In his book, Nouwen recounts how he was inspired by Rembrandt's painting of the same title. He shows how the three main characters of this Bible story all represent an aspect of each of us.

Most people primarily focus on the son who ran away from home with his inheritance and came back on hands and knees begging for forgiveness. It is a wonderful story of a Father's longing for His wayward child and a Grace that brings the lost home again. However, I would agree with Nouwen when he writes, "The father wants not only his younger son back, but his elder son as well. The elder son, too, needs to be found and led back into the house of joy."

How many times have we looked at the return of a "prodigal" and said to ourselves, "How nice! Another backslider has come back to the fold." We sit back with a self-righteous attitude and count our lucky stars that we've never let ourselves get mired in the lustful, unhealthy, deliberate sins of the flesh. That's how the eldest son felt.

"Now his older son was in the field. And as he came and drew near to the house, he heard music and dancing. So he called one of the servants and asked what these things meant. And he said to him, 'Your brother has come, and because he has received him safe and sound, your father has killed the fatted calf.'

But he was angry and would not go in. Therefore, his father came out and pleaded with him. So he answered and said to his father, 'Lo, these many years I have been serving you; I never transgressed your commandment at any time; and yet you never gave me a young goat, that I might make merry with my friends, but as soon as this son of yours came, who has devoured your livelihood with harlots, you killed the fatted calf for him!'" Luke 15: 25-30

Be honest with yourself. Do you ever feel the least bit resentful about being such a responsible, dependable person? Everyone can count on you to help out in a pinch and do the right thing. You carry the burden of setting a good example. You have always tried to do what it is that you "should" be doing. You've sacrificed for your family, worked hard at your job and made sure that you were involved in church. Does it ever just make you mad? Do you ever feel the urge to go out and do something "bad" just to spite everyone? Do you feel like you "deserve" God's blessings? After all, you pay your tithes and offerings and go to church every week. If you have ever felt any of these feelings, you are not alone. The story of the eldest son is for you–and me!

Listen to the Father's response: **"Son, you are always with me, and all that I have is yours!"** vs. 31

I like Henri Nouwen's response to those words: "The harsh and bitter reproaches of the son are not met with words of judgment. There is no recrimination or accusation. The father does not defend himself or even comment on the elder son's behavior. The father moves directly beyond all evaluations to stress his intimate relationship with his son. The father's declaration of unqualified love eliminates any possibility that the younger son is more loved than the elder. The father has shared everything with him. He has made him a part of his daily life, keeping nothing from him. There could be no clearer statement of the father's unlimited love for his elder son. The Father's unreserved, unlimited love is offered wholly and equally to both His sons. The return of the younger son makes him call for a joyful celebration. The return of the elder son makes him extend an invitation to full participation in the joy."

How you lost the joy? Perhaps you've never really experienced true joy to begin with. That may be because as we stand back looking at the return of our prodigal brother or sister, we are hearing a voice telling us that we are not the one that God really cares about. We tell ourselves that He is only interested in the "lost sheep". Why would God pay attention to the one who has never left home? And then we get whiny and think that perhaps God takes us for granted. "I am not His favorite child, therefore, I should not expect Him to give me what I really want." And most of all, we think, "I am not important enough to be found!" We feel lost, even though we've never left the house.

Henri Nouwen suggests that trust and gratitude can help us find our way home. "Acts of gratitude make one grateful because, step by step, they reveal that all is grace. But the true way home is through trust in Jesus, the eldest Son of God, who has come to show the Father's love and to free us from the bondage of our resentments." Let the Father welcome you home. Return to joy!

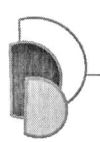

Choose for the Light

Darkness, despair
Confusion and hate
In the world
Seem to seal our fate.

But from the fog
Whispers a still, small voice,
"Look to Me,
Lift up your head
and rejoice!"

Don't wait until
You think all is well.
Make a choice,
In happiness dwell.

*Choose for the light
When darkness brings fear.
Choose for life
When death does appear.
Choose for truth
When surrounded by lies.
Choose for joy
In the midst of sad cries.*

One hidden act
Of repentance true,
One small word,
"Yes, I forgive you."

Random kindness,
One small gesture of love.
Brings God forth
From His bright
throne above.

He comes running
To welcome His own,
Arms outstretched,
"You're never alone!"

*Choose for the light
When darkness brings fear.
Choose for life
When death does appear.
Choose for truth
When surrounded by lies.
Choose for joy
In the midst of sad cries.*

—Linda

Choose Light

"And the city had no need
of the sun or of the moon
to shine for it, for the glory
of God illuminated it,
and the Lamb is its
light." Rev. 21:23

"Again, a new commandment
I write to you, which
thing is true in Him and
in you, because the
darkness is passing away,
and the true light is
already shining ...He who loves
his brother abides in the light, and
there is no cause for stumbling in
Him. " I John 2:10

"But you are a chosen
generation, a royal priesthood,
a holy nation, His own special
people, that you may

proclaim the praises of Him who called you out of darkness into His marvelous light." I Peter 2:9

"For you were once darkness, but now you are light in the Lord. Walk as children of light, for the fruit of the Spirit is in all goodness, righteousness, and truth, proving what is acceptable to the Lord." Eph. 5:8,9

"For it is the God who commanded light to shine out of darkness who has shone in our hearts to give the light of the knowledge of the glory of God in the face of Jesus Christ." 2 Corinthians 4:6

Temporary Insanity
Hormonal Dysfunctionality
Sporadic Days of Clarity
What is My Reality?

When I was a teen and spoke my mind or argued with my mother,
Someone would invariably shake their head and say with a knowing shudder,

"Its puberty she's going through. It's only just a stage.
Her hormones are the reason for her mood swings and outrage."

When my 20's came along, I was feeling fit and strong.
I would question my professors and tell my boyfriend he was wrong.
There were days of indecision and times of great distress,
And always someone to tell me, "It must be PMS!"

Then I entered into marriage and found myself with child.
There were many days of happiness and some days I was riled.
When I mourned the passing of my youthful shape or found myself in tears,
There was always someone ready to speak these words of cheer:

"Don't worry, dear. This soon will pass. Your hormones are the reason.

The baby blues will soon depart. They'll last for just a season."
In my middle and late 30's, life took on a hectic pace.
I fulfilled my wifely duties with a smile upon my face.
I nurtured, washed and fed the kids, and held a full time job.

But there were many times, I yelled and screamed and hung my head to sob. My spouse would frown and roll his eyes and say glumly with loud groans,
"It must be that time of month again, It's those darn, confounded hormones!"

I now stand deep in midlife, confused and feeling down.
Some days I think I'm losing it and I want to just leave town.
I wonder where I'm going and where I'm coming from. I go from feeling stupid to simply feeling numb.

When I confess my general turmoil, other folks just smile and nod,
"Don't worry dear, you need not fear. You're mind's not really flawed."
Then they pat my arm and wipe my brow and a quick wink they exchange.
"Now, now, don't fret. This too shall pass. You're just going through the change!"

Okay, I say. I'll accept my lot. It's the hormones I can blame.
But answer this, will you please? Is it really as you claim?

When this stage is passed and the pesky change dries up the hormones in my veins,
When I'm wrinkled, gray and stooped with age and full of aches and pains,

Will the mood swings stop? Will I smile again? Will sunshine flood my soul?
Will I not talk back? Will I never scream? Will I feel complete and whole?

Will I find at last the little child within, the one who's really me? If it's really true–then it sounds like heaven . . .

And that's likely where I'll be!

—Linda

Hormonal Dysfunctionality is not a phrase that you will find in the dictionary, but I would venture to guess that many women know exactly what it means. We all have those times of easy irritation, tears for no reason; days when we'd like to tear our hair out with frustration, and moments in which a loud shout would do the trick. But most of the time we cannot blame it on the hormones. It is just a fact of life that crises of all sizes will invariably come our way through every stage of our life. The tears, groans and shouts are just evidence of how we deal with them.

Crisis events come to us from many different sources. Some are a result of things beyond our control; the toilet overflows, the dog chews our best pair of shoes, a child falls and breaks an arm. Other times of stress come because of the normal transitions of life; we graduate into the working world, we marry and have children; we age and gain weight. And some times of crisis are a result of something that rises up within our souls. But no matter the reason, we tend to view any crisis event as a time of trouble and something very undesirable.

In the book, "When the Heart Waits," Sue Monk Kidd calls a crisis "a holy summons to cross a threshold. It involves both a leaving behind and a stepping toward, a separation and an opportunity." She suggests that most of us handle a crisis in one of two basic ways. We tell ourselves that it must be God's will and we therefore force ourselves into "an outwardly sweet acceptance, remaining unaffected at the deeper level of the spirit." The second way in which we tend to deal with stressful times is to "reject the crisis, fighting and railing against it until we become cynical and defeated or suffer a loss of faith."

Sue Monk Kidd offers a third way to face a crisis: "the way of waiting. This means creating a painfully honest and contemplative relationship with one's own depths, with God in the deep center of one's soul." In other words, a crisis can be an opportunity for spiritual growth and discovery. "Hope lies in braving the chaos and waiting calmly, with trust in the God who loves us. If we wait, we may find that God delivers us somewhere amazing, into a place vibrant with color and startling encounters with the soul."

There will always be days that you want to scream and shout and times when the tears will be threatening to spill. Troubles in all shapes and sizes will plague our days. And the hormones may rage. But through it all, remember that each crisis, no matter how big or small, is an opportunity for personal growth.

> **"Be of good courage, and He shall strengthen your heart, all you who hope in the Lord."**
> **Psalm 31:24**

Who Will Fight For Me?

She comes into the world
As a full blooming flower
With a heart thirsty for love
From her very first hour.

But cold hands of neglect
Crush fragile petals of trust
And a part of her withers
And turns into dust.

Despite days of
abandonment
And fear in the night
She thrives on
dewdrops of hope
And glimmers of light.

Yet, the tender,
young blossom
Is locked in a tower
Built with stones of distrust
And a misuse of power.

She waits for a knight
With his sword and
strong might
Who can break down
the strongholds
And make all things right.

"Won't you fight for me?"
Is the cry deep in her soul.
"Please delight in me,
Rescue me. Help
make me whole!"

A few brave ones attempt
To tear down the thick stone,
But they soon get
discouraged
And she's left all alone.

Her cries go unheeded
No one answers her pleas.
She's wounded and bleeding
And she falls to her knees.

It's then that she hears
A strong voice from above,
It's a voice filled
with promise
And laden with love.

"Stop looking below
For the answer to come.
Lift your face upward,
And look to the Son."

"Yes, I will fight for you
To My last dying breath.
Yes, I will rescue you
With my life-giving death."

"I'll continue to fight
With My mind, heart
and soul. I'll delight
in you, cherish you,
I'll make you whole."

So the beautiful rose
Turns her face to the sky
She's found her
prince charming,
On Him she'll rely.

—Linda

Maiden in Distress

According to John Eldredge in the book titled, "Wild at Heart", a man's heart is wired with three unique God-given needs:

- The need to be fierce and powerful.
- The need for adventures that test.
- The need to have a "beauty" to fight for.

In contrast, Eldredge says that, likewise, there are three things that the heart of a woman yearns for:

- The desire to be wanted and fought for.
- The desire to share in the adventure.
- The desire to be the beauty and to be delighted in.

In his book, he asks the question, "What is a Christian woman?" His answer: ". . . a Christian woman is tired. All we've offered the feminine soul is pressure to be a 'good servant.' No one is fighting for her heart, there is no grand adventure to be swept up in, and every woman doubts very much that she has any beauty to unveil."

Wow! Can you relate? I sure can. We grow up loving the fairy tale of the princess finding herself in trouble, only to be rescued by a knight in shining armor. And they live happily ever after. And oh, how disappointed we are! For somehow real life doesn't seem to work out that way. Abuse, neglect, put downs and criticism chip away at our tender, hopeful hearts. And unless a miracle happens and Someone comes along to rescue us, our hearts will turn to stone. But thank God for miracles:

> **"Then I will give them one heart, and I will put a new spirit within them.**
> **And take the stony heart out of their flesh, and give them a heart of flesh."**
> **Ezekiel 11:19**

Mortal man may fail us because he too, is a wounded soul searching for his heart's desire. The truth of the matter is that as long as men and women live on this earth, they will all be dealt deep wounding blows that will keep them from finding wholeness in one another.

And that is why we need a Savior. Only by opening up our wounded souls to God, will we be able to find that which will give us our heart's desire. It is only after that happens that we will find satisfaction and fulfillment in our earthly relationships.

Remember the beautiful word picture found in Ezekiel 16? This story of an abandoned young girl being rescued by the King is a wonderful reminder to us of God's powerful, rescuing love.

> **"And you became Mine, says the Lord . . .**
> **. . . You were exceedingly beautiful, and succeeded**
> **to royalty!"**

And they lived happily ever after . . .

Happily Ever After……

A young bride in the wedding of her dreams,
Knows she's found the answer to happily ever after
As she vows to love and cherish with the words, "I do."

But when the honeymoon is over and she steps down off cloud nine,
A chill of understanding dawns that perhaps it was a lie
And her dreams may not come true.

She pulls herself together and pushes away the doubt.
"Surely, to be a mom will fulfill my heart's desire!
I'll find real peace and joy at last!"

The children come and things speed up. Her life becomes a blur.
There's no time to think or worry about deep longings of her heart.
Her days just move too fast!

The kids grow into lives of their own.
She's left behind with a strange, quiet void and a
Kaleidoscope of feelings whirling around in her head.

It's true, her life's peaceful, but where is all the joy?
"Perhaps, when I'm a grandma with children to spoil and love . . ." She smiles and leaves the rest unsaid.

Linda Harris

Grandbabies come, not soon enough.
But long miles between and time apart disappoint.
Her weary heart strains for the dream that seems to tease and elude.

In a rare moment of stillness, the woman stands silent
Looking back over her life. "How did I miss it?
Where is this thing that I've chased and pursued?"

In the sunset of her life, understanding comes;
Happily ever after is really just a myth and
It doesn't really matter that its so.

The most important things in life are the issues of the
Heart and Soul; Life holds no guarantee for happiness or
riches. These things she comes to know.

What is certain in a woman's life is that she'll have
Her share of pain, along with failures, grief and losses,
And days of disappointment, fears and tears.

But through it all she can depend on this:
It's Hope that's kept her going and Faith that has sustained,
And it's Love that's been around her all these many years.

—Linda

A River Runs Through It

Like a boat on a river, our lives cut through the landscape of time. For miles we meander atop slow moving water. The view is peaceful and our thoughts sublime.

Then hopes and dreams urge us to paddle, to hurry downstream, our eyes on the future just round the bend. We've mapped out the voyage with high expectation and know for a fact just how it will end.

Without any warning, the boat starts to sway as it hits water that is foamy and white. Once clear depths, turn murky and rocky with more obstacles just out of sight.

Dark clouds cover us, winds of strife push us, as we are jostled and splashed with disagreement and pain. A quick view of rapids ahead brings desperation to change course, but we know it's in vain.

Our paddle is useless as we find ourselves in the midst of waters that churn and toss us about. We wonder if we should stay with the boat or would it be better to just jump out?

With a heart full of fear and a tight grip on the ship, we head through rough waters towards an unknown fork in our path. All hell seems to break loose and we face its full wrath. In our darkest moments, when all would seem lost, battered and bruised from our ordeal, we catch a glimpse of blue skies above and wonder if there is hope and if the calm below us is really what we feel.

We glance behind us and come to realize that it is true. We've past through the rapids and though not quite at ease, we take a deep breath and a sigh of relief as we see calm, placid waters just ahead through the trees.

On the river of life there are no guarantees, no definite prediction of a smooth sailing trip, but if we keep holding tight, hang on for the ride, live in the moment, stay with the ship,

The journey will teach us to embrace the adventure, learn from the past and relish the present. We can handle whatever the river will bring us, ready for truth, filled with assurance and more than content.

—Linda

Riding the Rapids

Not long ago, it was on my heart to call a dear friend to see how she was doing. I knew that she was experiencing many changes in her life and that she was very discouraged. As soon as I heard her voice, I could sense that she was depressed and drowning in a flood of conflicting emotions that were being churned up as important family relationships were undergoing transition. As we talked, I suddenly had a word picture form in my head that helped me "see" a bit of what she was experiencing. I could relate to the image because it had also been my own experience. I did my best to describe this word picture, praying that she would somehow find a glimmer of hope to hold on to.

In the days following our conversation I thought a lot about what we had talked about. The image that had come to mind was one of a woman alone in a rowboat that was being tossed and bounced along on rough, turbulent rapids. It was as if a flash flood had just occurred and she had been caught by surprise in a torrent of water rushing into the previously calm waters of her life. The angry waters had gathered dirt and debris, muddying the clear river, churning and hitting against the boat as it rushed wildly out of control down the fast moving current.

Whether or not it is the result of a forecasted storm or an unexpected downpour, the demise of any important relationship in our lives will most likely send us reeling and make us feel as if we are alone in a boat without paddles, rushing down category five rapids. In particular, changes in our marriage or with our children stir up large pieces of debris and dirt that are hurled at us, causing bruising and intense pain.

When you find yourself on this part of the river, it can be very difficult to think of anything other than the excruciating fear and pain. Sometimes the tendency at this point is to abandon ship. You want to jump overboard to try and reach shore and stop the fearful journey downstream. However dysfunctional the marriage or relationship has been doesn't seem to compare to the suffering your are going through in this moment. Oh, if only you could go back to where you were before! It couldn't be worse than this!

My friend was at this point. She was thinking that staying in her passionless marriage was better than experiencing the angst and turmoil she was currently going through. I remember briefly feeling this way through my own divorce. Why was I rocking the boat? What was wrong with the status quo? Did I really want to be another failed marriage statistic? Wouldn't it be better for the kids if we stayed together? Is it worth all of this pain? Would I really be happier living alone?

In the end, I decided to stay in the boat and face what I might find downstream with the hope that things would eventually smooth out.

It wasn't my intention to urge my friend to go through with ending her marriage, but I did want to remind her that in time, her pain would subside. The river would settle down and the debris would thin out and disperse. I encouraged her to look to the horizon, past the dark, gray clouds to the sliver of light far in the distance.

Riding the rapids means going with the flow. The demise of any relationship will be painful. The unknown change it may bring to our lives can be frightening. However, I have learned that if we allow it to happen, the end of a relationship will inevitably bring about new beginnings in our lives. While the process of change can be very tumultuous, things WILL calm down and smooth out for us as long as we let go, accept the change and hold on tight while running the rapids.

With a bit of courage and strength from above, you may even find yourself feeling excitement, adventure and a surprising sense of anticipation to see what is around the next bend or over the next set of rolling rapids. Hold on to hope, keeping in mind that smooth waters ARE ahead.

You will reach shore where you can confidently step out on the highway of life. Ah . . . but one small warning to heed. Even on this new road, be ready to expect some delays along the way. Embrace them and learn!

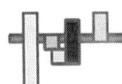

High Hopes

Traveling along with high hopes
On a road full of expectations,
You end up in a deep ditch
Of disappointment and frustration.

You wonder where you went wrong,
How did you miss the warning signs?
When did you cross on over
The solid yellow lines?

Was it when you sat and waited
For the telephone to ring?
Or when you looked into the mailbox
And didn't find a thing?

Was it when your birthday came and went
And your daughter did not call?
Or when you cooked that special meal
And received no thanks at all?

The expectation highway
Is known to twist and turn,
And if you are not careful,
You might just crash and burn.

Linda Harris

The expectation highway
Is a dangerous place to be.
It toys with your emotions
And does not let you see.

You feel helpless, then so hopeful,
The anticipation soars,
Opportunity comes knocking
But you slam against locked doors!

Around the bend a roadblock
Changes every thoughtful plan.
You have to turn around
And go back where you began.

The journey down the road of life
Is a hazard from the start.
So buckle up your hopes and dreams
Hold them tight within your heart.

—Linda

High Hopes
"Be of good courage,
And He shall strengthen your heart,
All you who Hope in the Lord."
Psalm 31:24

Like a young child eagerly anticipating Christmas, we have all felt the excitement of anticipation that comes with hoping and waiting for something to happen. From fantasizing about holding the winning lottery ticket to the joyful expectation of a visit from a loved one, we have all found ourselves in a state of hope.

And invariably, we have been knocked down with disappointment. How many times have we waited by the phone, never to hear it ring or hoped for a promotion never to have it materialize? The let-down that packs the most punch usually involves a personal relationship. Promises are made and then broken. A romantic evening is planned, but the reality is an argument over dinner. Confidences are shared in a developing new friendship, but trust is shattered with careless words. Unrealized expectations always hurt.

Unfortunately, there is no way to guarantee that the road of life on earth will be free of disappointments. However, there is one relationship in which we can put our hope and one in which we can trust that all will turn out as anticipated:

"Thus God, determining to show more abundantly to the heirs of promise, the immutability of His counsel, confirmed it by an oath, that by two immutable things, in which it is impossible For God to lie, we might have strong consolation, who have fled for refuge to **lay hold of the Hope set before us. This hope we have as an anchor of the soul, both sure and steadfast,** *and Which enters the Presence behind the veil, where the forerunner has entered for us,* **even Jesus, Having become High Priest forever."***
Hebrews 6:18-20

Despite the bumps and obstacles that get in our way, we **can** hold fast to Jesus, knowing that He will **never** let us down.

At times, it is our hope in Christ which is the only thing that keeps us from falling off the cliff of despair. So grab on with all your might and hold tight with all your heart!

> **"Now may the God of hope fill you with all joy and peace in believing, that you may abound In hope by the power of the Holy Spirit." Romans 15:13**

"It Was God's Will."

These words have always been difficult for me. The issue of knowing God's will has been pondered by many people for a long time. Many want to know exactly what God has planned for them. They want to be sure that they make the "right" decisions.

I remember as I was growing up, several occasions in which our family made life changing moves because my father thought that it was God's will that he take a certain job that had come up. I've heard stories of people who woke up one morning and cancelled their travel plans, to later find out that the plane or train they were scheduled to be on crashed. They believed that they were spared because it was God's will. I always use to think about all those other people who still kept their travel plans and died that day! What about them?

We've all heard of someone telling a grieving mother, "It was God's will. Your child is safe in the arms of Jesus now." In the church I grew up in, I remember conversations that centered around the death of someone and invariably it would be announced that "God knew to take that person now…because if they had lived longer, maybe they would have strayed and not been saved."

In the Psalms, King David talks about God directing or illuminating our paths. Many of us have read these texts and thought . . . ."Aha…this must mean that God has a specific plan for me and it is up to me to find out what that plan is."

I would like to suggest another thought. God's government is set up so that all of us have freedom of choice.

This means that we humans make choices that have exponential ramifications for all of us. Imagine the surface of a still pond. Throw a pebble into it and watch the rings move out from the point of impact. Then think of a handful of pebbles being thrown into it. The result is a wide area of intersecting paths and options of travel.

Throughout our lives, we cross many such paths. These paths have not all been designed by God. He didn't throw the pebbles, we did. What I am saying is that I don't believe God constructs the road that goes before us. But He DOES walk the road we choose right alongside of us. The miracle of God working in our lives is that He guides us and helps us traverse the many crisscrossing paths that we come to.

The important factor is one that is very intrinsic, rather than external. God is not outside of us working construction or directing us with signs along the way. He lives IN us, and if we really listen, we will know that He is there to guide us through the mazes of our life.

This is not to say that God cannot put up detours, build bridges or fill in potholes. He IS GOD after all.

However, when the Bible talks about God completing a good work within us, that is exactly what it is—IN us! He does soul construction, not road construction.

To Break Free

Desires, thoughts and ideas
Swirl around and strain against their fleshy shell,
But somehow they fail
To evoke emotion and escape their facial cell.

Lord, I'm a prisoner of my body and I want to break free!
When You look deep inside me, what do you see?

I'm a soul longing to soar high into the warmth of Your light,
Free, unencumbered, the flesh out of sight!

I want to break free of the darkness that stalks me,
To feel weightless, unburdened, O Lord, can it be?

My soul longs to taste passion, natural and true.
My heart yearns to explode with laughter and joy
And intimately feel the presence of You!

—Linda

Liberation!

"O wretched (wo)man that I am! Who will deliver
me from this body of death?" Romans 7:24

This may sound strange, but there are times that I would love to shed my body and let my soul fly free! The flesh, at times, feels so restrictive and cumbersome! It takes a lot of energy to maintain and much too much time is spent trying to shrink it, transform it, or cover it up! As I get older, the aging body starts to creak and groan. I have this fantasy that in heaven, I will only be shrouded in a robe of light that is weightless and easily molded to the shape I want! No more worries about weight gain, blemishes or achy bones.

When one reads the writings of Paul, it seems apparent the he also had a desire to be rid of his earthly flesh:

> *"For in this we groan, earnestly desiring to be clothed with our habitation which is from heaven,*
> *If indeed, having been clothed, we shall not be found naked.* **For we who are in this tent groan, being burdened,** *not because we want to be unclothed, but further clothed, that mortality may be swallowed up by life ....* **We are confident, yes, well pleased rather to be absent from the body and to be present with the Lord.**
> *2 Corinthians 5:5-8*

Paul didn't just want to be rid of his earthly body, he had a longing to be intimate with God. Have you noticed how some people spend most of their lives trying to cover up who they are inside? They refuse to acknowledge their feelings or listen to what their heart is telling them. However, when we come to know Christ and His Spirit woos our own spirit, a deep longing for intimacy with God wells up within. We want to be open and vulnerable to God's Spirit. We wish that our heart's desire—our dreams and ideas—would be fully understood by Him.

While on this earth, we keep hoping that an earthly relationship will bring us this kind of intimacy. I do believe that God's original purpose for the sexual union between a man and a woman was to be a spiritual example for us—one which would give us a taste of the intimacy that God wants with each of us. When the Bible says that "Adam knew Eve", the Hebrew word used has to do with discernment, understanding and being endued with the other. This "knowing" was to be more than just a physical act. Because of sin, however, this act has become warped and many times despite our desire, we are never quite satisfied; we never quite feel understood by the other. A hungry hole still resides within us and it happens to be a God-sized hole which only God in us can fill up. The ironic thing is that in order for this to happen, God had to clothe Himself in the body of a human! He poured Himself into a body so that we could one day break out of ours!

I Am Not My Body

The essence of myself
Is held captive within its frame,
But I am not my body.

The first organ of life
Beats in rhythm and pumps blood
Through artery and vein,
But it is not the true heart of the matter.

Synapses spark, endorphins rush
And flood the brain,
But my thoughts escape.
I am not my body.

Muscles stretch and ache with wear,
Bones bend and sometimes break.
Nerves cry out in protest,
But my will survives.

It tries to betray me,
Squeeze me with pain,
Change shape, wrinkle and grow weak,
But I am not my body.

Who I am transcends skin and bone,
I'm a soul temporarily trapped
In mortal flesh,
A spiritual being, in tune to something
Bigger than myself, another dimension.

I am a spirit of determination and strength.
I carry hurts, prejudice and a
Myriad of emotions within my heart,
But I am not my body.

You may subdue it, abuse it
And destroy it,
But I am not my body and
Who I am can never be erased.

For while it may die and return to dust,
Who I am is held in trust by
The God, who knows
I am not my body!

—Linda

Be Still!

I didn't even know I stood in darkness
Until the veil was lifted from my soul,
Suddenly revealing I really was not whole.

As the curtain pulled away and light came flooding in,
It was then I saw the chains, rusty with hurt,
Imprisoning my heart with cruel restrain.

In rising panic, I strained and pulled
Against the bindings that cruelly held me tight.
Twisting, I fought to break free,
Struggling with all my might.

But chains of pain, disapproval and pride
Had been forged together with anger hot.
The links could not be loosened,
No matter how I fought.

Overwhelmed with despair,
Trembling in fear of confinement,
With tears, I cried out, "God, I'm through!
Lord, you've shown me the Truth,

But what can I do?"

It was in that moment of helplessness
That gentle words fell with a quieting touch,
"My daughter, stand still.
I want to show you so much!"

Hope filled my heart as I heard what He said,
"This fight is not yours, it is Mine - don't you see?
With praise, ask and believe and I'll set you free!"

With a sigh and deep breath, I stood very still
And knew that for me to do nothing was best.
"Exactly, my child!" He said.
"I Am your rest!"

—Linda

M.Whiting

My Prayer

> "For Behold, I am for you
> And will turn to you
> And you shall be tilled and sown."
> Ezekiel 36:9

Lord, please work the earth of my heart,
Break up the fallow ground.
Thrust your spade in deep,
Where long-rooted weeds of neglect are found.

Till the soil where perceived hurts
Have nourished prickly thorn.
Break through the crusty surface,
Dig out the stones of pride and scorn.

Refresh with Your Spirit.
Plant seeds of faith and love.
Nourish with care and compassion.
Send showers of hope from above.

Let me grow strong in Your Grace
With my roots anchored deep,
Standing firm in Your word
With bountiful fruit ready to reap.

—Linda

The Beatitudes

Blessed are the poor in spirit,
For theirs is the kingdom of heaven.
Blessed are those who mourn,
For they shall be comforted.
Blessed are the meek,
For they shall inherit the earth.
Blessed are those who hunger and thirst
for righteousness,
For they shall be filled.
Blessed are the merciful,
For they shall obtain mercy.
Blessed are the pure in heart,
for they shall see God.
Blessed are the peacemakers,
For they shall be called sons of God.
Blessed are those who are persecuted for
righteousness sake,
For theirs is the kingdom of heaven.
Matthew 5

—Linda

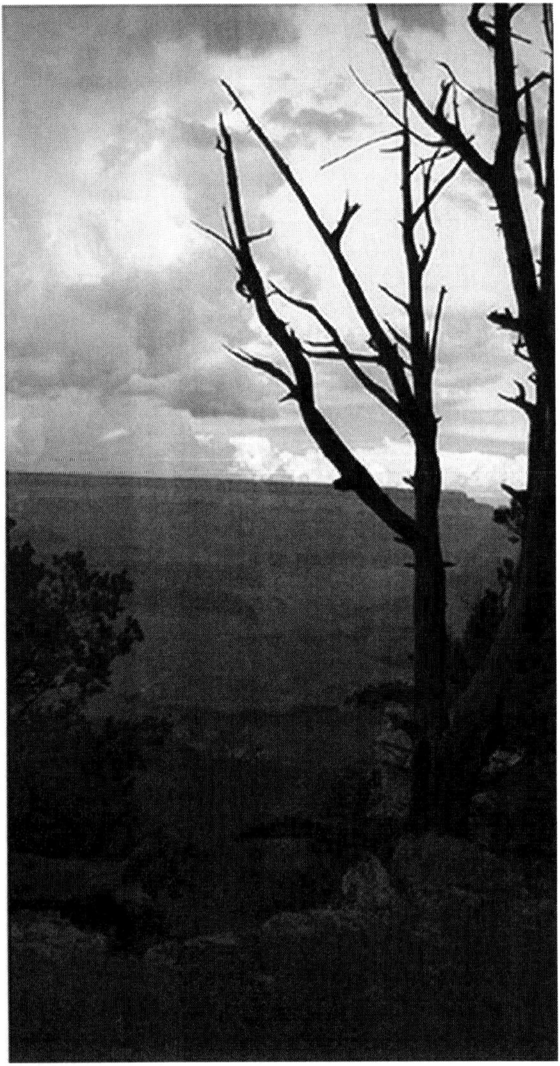

I Know You!

The Beatitudes of Matthew 5 are very familiar verses to anyone who has read the Bible. These words from Christ's sermons on the mount are meant to be an inspiration to his followers. I have to admit to you, however, that these words always left me feeling somewhat discouraged.

I suppose one reason that I didn't fully appreciate these poetic words of Jesus was that I was coming from the mindset that I had to be perfect in order to be saved. I heard these words to say that if I was going to ever make it to heaven that I must be a meek, merciful peacemaker who was pure in heart and could be expected to be persecuted! Reading the list of attributes that Christ mentions in these verses, weighed me down with the regret that I could never measure up to all these saintly characteristics.

I thought I could lay claim to a few of these qualities. I knew I could be merciful, but I certainly wasn't meek! (My family could certainly confirm that fact!) As for pure in heart, what did that even look like?

Having finally discovered the truth about God's amazing Grace and understanding that there is nothing whatsoever that I can do to obtain salvation, I can look at the Beatitudes from a new perspective. I realize that all these qualities come only from God. However, even with this knowledge, I have come to see the words from Christ's sermon in a much different light.

I like to imagine that Jesus was not giving us a list of characteristics that we must display, but rather He was making a point of talking in a personal way to each and every personality found in mankind. He was making sure that every person felt spoken to. He wanted all to know that they were valued by Him. His words showed that he could see deep into everyone's soul and meet the needs of each and every heart. There was a blessing for ALL!

Blessed Are You

Today, I say to you who are of
Compliant, Melancholy personality,
Blessed are you, the poor in spirit.
I recognize your struggle for self,
Your feelings of depression.
You look at the world and feel
hopelessness at its condition.
But I tell you, take heart!
The Kingdom of Heaven is yours–Now!
I know how you mourn your failings
And feel deeply the
sorrows of the world,
To you, I give you My Comfort.

Jesus turns and looks toward the
back to catch a woman's eyes.

She shyly glances down……
Blessed are you who are meek.

You are content to be in the background.
Blessed are you the Peacemakers.
You are a personality of Steadiness and Loyalty.
You desire peace and stability.
I want to offer you reassurance.
You will be given the land.
It is your rightful inheritance as the children of God.

The Master looks down to a young
man in front of Him.........

And to you, the Choleric, the one who shows
a Dominance personality,
I know how you thirst and hunger
after truth and righteousness.
You have a deep hole in your soul.
Your quest to quench your thirst
Sometimes hurts yourself and others,
But I recognize the tender longings of your soul.
Drink of Me–the Living Water.
You Shall Be Filled!
That is My guarantee.

Jesus smiles and looks lovingly at a young
woman at His feet. Then He says......

Linda

To you who love people, the ones of Influencing personalities,
You have a gift of mercy.
Blessed are you.
You, too, desire peace and harmony.
And yet you fear rejection and struggle with insecurity.
Be of good cheer. You are sons and daughters of God!
You will obtain mercy. You will not be rejected by Me!

Then Jesus scans the crowd. As a loving Father
to His children He continues . . .

If for My sake any of you are persecuted or reviled;
If men try to speak evil against you,
Remember who you are!
You are My children!
Rejoice in that knowledge. Be exceedingly glad!
I love you just as you are right now.

Linda

Through a Glass Darkly

I've spent my life looking at God through a microscope
My view being something finite and measurable,
A list of rules and standards, small parts of a whole with definite boundaries and borders of confinement.
An observer bigger than that being observed,
And yet, like a barnacle on a whale,
Blissfully unaware of the entirety of my universe.
I felt empowered, thinking I could manipulate and control what I saw, and yet fearful that I would fail
And the microscopic organism under scrutiny
Would be the death of me.

Then God's Grace knocked me off my feet.
On the ground, I was forced to look up through the lens of a telescope, Getting a glimpse of something infinite and immeasurable.
I've since put my eye to the scope and have seen vast expanses of God's love, limitless, with no boundaries.
I am powerless and know that there is nothing out there that I can control. I am an insignificant speck in the context of what is being observed.

And yet, I know that I matter, for He who is the beginning and the end, the Alpha and Omega, knows who I am.
And while I am nothing, I am everything to Him,
For He, who is infinite, became a barnacle for a moment in time So that I could one day see the entirety of God's universe And know that eternal life was my destiny.

—Linda

Listening

Have you ever wondered how the God of endless space can discern the minute pleas of your own longing heart? I would imagine that in those rare moments when God takes a breath and just listens to the voices of earth, that He hears a loud cacophony rising up to meet Him. A confusion of sounds must rush up from the dark spaces of this egotistical sphere; voices of despair and torment, mingling with the muffled cries of broken hearts.

It hardly seems possible that a single voice can be heard above the din of anger that swirls upward like poisonous smog from a polluted planet.

And yet I know this: As He bends His ear closer, God can distinguish the small pinpoints of praise from the sighs of sad souls. For His ears are fine tuned to the call of each individual being. His sweet spirit moves like a soft breeze, wooing and soothing His endangered creation.

And I would imagine that if one would only stop and stand still for one quiet breath in time that the penetrating whisper of God's voice could be heard. In the midst of destruction and despair a message of hope is made audible to the heart.

> "You are my children and I hear your voice.
> I will never leave you nor forsake you, For I am with
> you always and forever."

The Road Leading Home

Little girl lost,
Struggling to find her way home
In the swirling mist of narrow expectations
And unacceptance,
She continues to roam.

Little girl afraid,
But pushing forward in blind haste,
Trying so hard to prove herself worthy, yet always falling short.
A deep fear she must taste.

Little girl wounded,
Confusing biting criticism for something familiar and right,
Abandoning self-respect in the silencing of her heart's desire, she wants to give up the fight.

Little girl wandering,
Through a maze of subtle lies,
Getting hooked by the barbs of deceit and misguided advice.
Something in her soul dies.

Linda

Little girl weary,
Hears a soft voice call out her name,
She stops and stands still, peering hard into the fog.
Has something just shifted or is it all just the same?

Little girl hopeful,
Sees the grey veil start to part,
A light breaks through the darkness,
Giving her a glimpse of the road leading home,
That place that lies buried deep in her heart.

—Linda

Home is Where the Heart Is

"Above all else, guard your heart, for it is the wellspring of life." Proverbs 4:23

A healthy, new baby has no pretense. While it can sometimes be difficult to decipher a baby's "language", the little ones do a great job of expressing themselves naturally from the core of their being. No game playing. They just let it all out as they feel it. However, it doesn't take long for external influences to push and shape and even squelch a young one's natural responses. I remember with my own children, how often I would catch them looking at my face, trying to gauge my reaction to their behavior. They would listen carefully to conversations around them, trying to take it all in. They quickly learned what would get them positive or negative responses. They internalized these reactions and learned quickly that it could be important for their well-being to squelch certain impulses, words or actions.

This kind of learning is important for children in many ways because it helps them learn to get along in society, to temper their impulsiveness and to have a sense of what is considered right or wrong. It certainly makes living with other people easier! However, despite its importance, the many voices of expectation, criticism and judgment that each of us are exposed to over our lifetime can be quite damaging at times. Think back on your own life. Can you see any defining moments in which your own voice, the cry of your heart, was overruled or worse, stomped on by another louder one?

It may have been the constant look of disapproval or anger on a parent's face or the seemingly underserved slap or spanking you got. Perhaps the religion of your youth gave you the impression that you had to work very hard to gain God's approval, that you just weren't good enough as you were. It may have been something simple like a chance remark that made reference to a supposed flaw on your body or in your character. Maybe you were bullied or made fun of by classmates. Perhaps you felt as if you never measured up to the expectations of a lover or spouse and it seemed as if you were the one always blamed for any misunderstandings or conflicts in the relationship.

These things happen to all of us. The point here is not to lay blame upon the people that may have had a part in the squelching of our voices or the hurt inflicted on our hearts. Each of them were responding from their own ignorance and pain. I am guilty of doing this myself, although I hate to admit it! The point is to acknowledge these things in our life and learn to listen once again to the newborn heart within each of us.

I would venture to guess that if you took some time to look back on your life, you would see those times in which your heart tried to tell you what was truth about yourself, someone else or God. You probably felt a little niggle of warning or a welling up of joy as your heart attempted to make a connection with your brain about a particular someone or circumstance. And how many times, because of those old distorted recordings in our heads, did we ignore what our heart was trying to tell us? I would guess it has happened far too often. The sad fact is, that each time we squelch that inner voice, it becomes harder to discern.

Over the last decade, my life has fallen into the textbook pattern of looking back. My quest for meaning and truth has led me to examine many things. I have spent hours pondering my childhood, religion, spirituality, marriage and friendships. This introspection has been very valuable and has taught me several important lessons. The most vital thing that I've learned is that I CAN indeed trust my heart. With the perspective of time, I can now clearly see those times when my heart was trying to tell me something that I counted as mere fancy or silly, distorted emotion, when in fact it was speaking absolute truth.

In many ways, I feel as if I've spent much of my life walking through a thin veil of mist. I suppose that is what Paul is talking about in I Corinthians 13:12: "Now we see things imperfectly as in a poor mirror, but then we will see everything with perfect clarity. All that I know now is partial and incomplete, but then I will know everything completely, just as God knows me now."

"Just as God knows me now." I like that! God knows me from the inside out. He's with me on this journey of self-discovery, the slicing through the fog, layer by layer. The way home is through Him and He is in my heart.

On This Day...

One this day, I walk with confidence, my head held high,
On top of the world, sure I'll accomplish whatever I try.
From the inside looking out, I see potential up ahead,
My step is light, my focus clear, I know exactly where I'll tread.

A sudden glance in a window I pass by, stops me cold,
A woman stares back at me, a bit worn out and looking old.
Her tired eyes quickly look away, as if afraid I'll see inside.
But it's too late, a slowly dawning truth comes and cannot hide.

I turn and walk through the door of self-doubt and self-hate,
Quickly I want to cover myself before it's too late!
Who am I to think I can strut, that I have something to share?
Incriminations dance through my head. How do I dare?

Stumbling through a maze of confusion, I trip over my pride.
I lose my poise and my once sure footing and begin to slide.
A firm hand stops my fall. "Let me help," is whispered in my ear.
I turn and see His kind, smiling face and hear, "Do not fear."
You've come to the right place. I've been waiting for you!
Let me give you a makeover and show you what's true."

With loving hands, He performed His magic, then dressed me in white, He stood me in front of His mirror to take in the sight.

Afraid to look, with eyes closed tight, the truth I was unwilling to face. No make-up could hide the fact that I was undeserving of any grace. "My child, open your eyes and look at the beautiful woman I see.
It's nothing that's earned, but it's solely a gift from Me!"

I peeked and then opened my eyes wide, amazed at what I saw,
The woman who peered back at me, stood tall without a flaw.
"Looking from the outside to deep within, this is who you are,
My creation, clothed in My redeeming love, My shining star."

—Linda

The Gift of Something We Love

> "Self-Hatred seems to me an evil thing in itself
> Rather than an antidote to evil.
> If we practice self-hatred, then the sacrifice we
> make of ourselves and our lives is not sacred, for it
> is then a gift of something we hate rather than of
> something that we have nurtured and loved."
> (from: Confessions of a Pagan Nun
> by Kate Horsely)

The idea that I must love myself has been a difficult concept for me to grasp. I do not think that I am alone in this struggle. Anyone who has been raised under the influence of an authoritative religious environment knows that self-love is not an aspect of character development that we are encouraged to strive for! I remember being taught the acronym: J.O.Y.–Jesus, Others, You!

It sounds so noble and honorable to spout such a concept. Putting myself last would seem to be the "Christian" thing to do, however, I have come to realize that this is a very deceptive and damaging belief. For women in particular, much harm has come from the idea that we must avoid self-love.

Because we feel as if we are worthless, we make poor decisions in our life. We fail to listen to our hearts and the wise intuition that God put within us. That niggling voice that tells us to avoid a situation or relationship is squelched because we doubt ourselves. After all, we must put everyone else ahead of ourselves. That means we ignore what we want and need. Ultimately, this breeds anger and resentment. This hurts us individually and those whom we love.

I find it ironic that in my own life, it was the influence of a woman who cultivated my own self-hatred. A dead woman, whose prolific words filled my brain with the idea that putting myself first was sinful and dangerous for my eternal welfare. A wonderful result of leaving behind the church of my childhood and its "prophetess" has been the realization that I am truly worthy of God's love. Not worthy because of anything I have done, but valued and beloved by God just because I am His own daughter, His creation!

When we have accepted Christ as our Savior and believe that His Spirit dwells within our hearts, then the idea of putting oneself first is NOT dangerous! Insisting that we be last in everything; that we put other people's needs before our own, only denigrates that which God has deemed worthy of His love and indwelling Spirit. It is in fact, a kind of twisted egotism. How dare we despise the person whom

God has redeemed with His blood and resurrection?!

It is only when we understand our value and know that we are truly loved just as we are, that we can be of any good to the rest of the world. That knowledge is what brings us peace and contentment and allows us to be a blessing to those around us.

> "God saved you by his special favor
> when you believed.
> And you can't take credit for this,
> it is a gift from God.
> Salvation is not a reward for the good things
> we have done,
> So none of us can boast about it.
> **For we are God's masterpiece!**
> He has created us anew in Christ Jesus,
> So that we can do the good things
> He planned for us long ago."
> Ephesians 2:8-10

Don't be afraid to love yourself! You are God's masterpiece!! The results of loving yourself will be that you will take care of yourself. You will guard your heart and listen to your intuition. Loving yourself will bring you healthy relationships. Most of all, it will bring you contentment and a sense of satisfaction that what you have to offer the world is a wonderful gift from God!

A Peaceful Place

We journeyed to a peaceful place,
Myself and three dear friends.
We left the cares of life behind
With hopes that hearts would mend.

Sheltered in a cottage quaint
And beside the ocean blue,
We explored the past and present
With friends we knew were true.

With gentle words and cleansing tears
We found a safe place there.
With open hearts we searched our souls
And shared ourselves in prayer.

In longing for a heavenly place
It soon became so clear,
God's Kingdom was before us
In each friend we held so dear.

LINDA HARRIS

Our time together soon did end.
We had to say good-bye.
With parting words and promises
We tried hard not to cry.

Our peaceful journey brought us joy
And memories very dear.
A source of strength and comfort that will
Keep each other near.

—Linda

Friendship: Bringing Light to the Blind

There is a sweet story about a dog and a cat who were survivors of Hurricane Katrina. These animals had been left behind in the confusion of people being quickly rescued from their flooded houses. The dog was tied to the front porch of the house with a chain and food and water were left by the owners who were hoping they could come back soon for their beloved pets. Weeks passed and no one was allowed back into the neighborhood. In desperation, the dog finally broke free and with her chain dragging the ground she and her calico friend took off looking for nourishment.

Four months later, the pair were rescued and taken to a temporary animal shelter that had been set up by volunteers. The volunteers tried to separate the animals, but they would not have it. The dog whined and barked all night and would not settle down until the cat was brought into the cage with her. It was then discovered that the cat had a disability. He was blind!

One can only wonder what struggles the animals had to endure in the months they were on their own. But it is clear that they took care of each other and that their companionship kept them going. It is a beautiful story of friendship and support. (From: "The Two Bobbies" by Larson, Nethry and Cassels)

This story is an obvious illustration of how important friendship can be. There are so many times in my life in which my friends helped keep me on the path of sanity! The constancy of a friend's love and support is something to be treasured beyond all things. The one aspect of this story that got me thinking, however, was the idea of "blindness" in connection to friendship.

There is a story in the Bible found in John 9 which tells about how Jesus healed a blind man and how the religious leaders had such a difficult time with this miracle. Jesus told them that He had come to give sight to the blind and to show those who think they see that they are blind. The religious gurus responded in total shock at His words and asked Him, "Are you saying that we are blind?" Jesus' response was, "If you were blind, you wouldn't be guilty. **But you remain guilty because you claim you can see!**"

My pondering heart is struck by those words! So many times we journey through life completely oblivious to our own lack of sight. We gather people around us in the name of friendship who help us keep the illusion alive. We think we know who we are and what we are about. We convince ourselves that we are justified in our thoughts and actions and we make sure that we bring people into our life who will either distract us from thinking too deeply or who will pander to our self-delusion with their words and actions. That is not true friendship.

In my own life, I have been blessed with many wonderful friends. These friends do love me unconditionally and boost my ego with their words of appreciation and support. However, the friends that I hold the dearest to my heart are those who go a step further and help me probe the blindness of my heart. This is not an easy thing to do. The natural tendency for most of us is to avoid conflict. We don't want to come across as being judgmental or unaccepting in our friendships and as a result we sometimes let things go unsaid. My best friends have taken the risk and in love, helped me explore the dark, murky places of my heart with the light of their friendship. They have helped me see aspects of myself that I have previously ignored. They have done this in a way that has made me feel safe in the discovery process.

My closest friends have also helped me uncover lies that I have believed about myself and helped me replace them with truth. Each of us has come in contact with people who can with a single word or action send an arrow of self-doubt and recrimination deep into our souls. A chance remark about a physical feature, a teasing, hurtful joke implying some deficiency in our character or an accusation thrown in our face can pierce us and plant little lies into the depths of our hearts. Over time, these lies fester and grow into warped beliefs about ourselves that can create havoc in our lives.

As I've looked back over my life, I've been amazed at how many lies I had come to believe about myself as a result of my dysfunctional marriage. It can be difficult to see dysfunction when you are smack dab in the middle of it. Since my divorce, I've been able to recognize certain fallacies that I have accepted as truth in my own life. It is my dearest friends who have helped me through the process of identifying a deceit and replacing it with the actual truth of the matter. I will be forever grateful for their willingness to go deep with me on this journey of self-discovery! The irony is that these friends are not always deliberate in their help. Something they say offhand shines a light on a particular aspect of my belief system. I am stunned by the awareness of seeing the truth about myself–a truth that has always been there, but that I failed to recognize because I allowed another person's dysfunction to become my own.

I thank God for the wonderful friends that He has brought in to my life. I am a woman greatly blessed with friendship. In my blindness, He has given me light through His Spirit and through the friends He has given me.

GPS

Go Lightly
Pay Attention
Savor the Experience

Go lightly, tread softly,
Some things are best left as they are.
Let go, let be, don't try to change,
Just learn to walk away.

Pay close attention, Be alert,
Who knows what you might see ?
Beauty, truth, and something new,
There's meaning in every day.

Savor, relish, just enjoy,
Experience the present moment.
Live in the now, accept the grace,
You'll find joy is in the play.

—Linda

Go Lightly!

As some who know me can attest, I am a woman who likes to dig deep and probe relentlessly into hearts and minds. This is close to being a curse because all that excavating can create havoc for me and others that I come in contact with. While I'm thinking that it can only be healthy to do a little archeological work, not all would agree with me. Especially those that come in close contact with my probing tools!

I've also been one to work hard at mending and mediating relationships that aren't quite working. I hate misunderstanding and over the years have done my best to smooth any relational conflict out. I suppose there is real irony in that since my deep digging philosophy has created some of those conflicts. I've just clung to the idea that if we just all hang in there and work through the problems, despite the pain, that things will be okay. Very naïve on my part, I suppose.

That said, I am finding as I begin the journey into middle age that I've run out of energy to put into those dysfunctional relationships. I am finding that I am a bit indifferent and not as willing to push through the hard stuff, particularly if a relationship has turned toxic. This indifference has bothered me. It's a new emotion that doesn't fit well. However, a recent conversation with a dear friend has helped me to see that perhaps there is something to be learned from this indifference. Perhaps it is time that I learn to GO LIGHTLY!

To "go lightly" involves letting go of relationships that are just not working and letting them be. It means that I will be cordial and polite, but I will not try and fix the relationship. I will stay on the surface of emotions and stay away from dangerous topics. I will give up my own expectations for what a proper relationship should look like. I will not push for deep discussion, but rather I will cultivate my own weak skills at small talk and chit-chat. I will do my best to be quiet and listen. This leads me to step #2 of my GPS………

Pay Attention!

"Attention is the intention to live without reservation in the here and now."

—Timothy Miller

"Everything in life itself is speaking, is audible, is communicating, in spite of its apparent silence."

—Poet Hazrat Inayat Knan

Paying attention is a deliberate act of being aware. In order to do this best, one needs to be quiet and listen. It is a matter of using our senses to observe three basic aspects of life: THINGS, PEOPLE and SELF.

When we take the time to observe our environment, we can find meaning in the simplest things. Think of all the ways a flower inspires us. In a flower we see love and romance, wonder and beauty, and a view of the great cycle of our lives. The authors of the book, "Spiritual Literacy" , suggest that everything in our life can be a source of meaning and even sacredness. "Be prepared to look long and steadily at things. They will speak to you and reveal themselves … moments of grace, epiphanies, and great insights are lost to us because we are in too much of a hurry to notice them. Slow down or you'll miss the good stuff." (pg. 53)

Sometimes in those moments in which we are being an observer of our world, we simply enjoy a triggered memory that has meaning to us. There can be much joy in remembering. Once upon a time in my own life, I spent several years living on a tropical island, 6,000 miles from home. One Christmas, I remember standing in the open pavilion of the island's airport sending someone home for the holidays. In the midst of saying goodbye and greeting people who were coming off the plane, I caught a whiff of something familiar to me, but foreign to the island. I turned and looked to see a Christmas tree being carted through the lobby. It was just your average pine tree, not too big, but I wanted to run over and put my arms around it and bury my nose in its needles.

Several of the American kids who were with me all had the same idea. It wasn't long before a little crowd had gathered around that poor person and their tree, oohing and ahhing as we stuck our noses in the branches and breathed deeply of the pine scent. You would have thought we were tasting the most delicious of foods or watching a fantastic fireworks display for all the sounds of awe we were making. That unique smell of Christmas took us all back to wonderful times with our families who were so far away from us that particular season. I remember being surprised at how a simple smell could trigger a flood of emotion and warm thoughts.

As I look around this little room in which I am writing, I see several small objects that remind me of someone or something of value in my life. I've never been one to cling to "stuff". In fact, for me, getting rid of things can be very therapeutic! At the same time, even when I am in a mood to purge myself from the clutter that sometimes piles up around me, I am careful to keep certain items that hold special meaning for me. Paying attention to those things can turn the ordinary into something special and meaningful.

The next aspect of deliberate attention giving can be the most difficult for many us; paying attention to people. This doesn't just mean sitting in a mall watching everyone as they walk by. (Although, that can be quite an interesting learning experience!) It involves learning to really listen to words and the body language of those we come in contact with. So many times, we get involved in a discussion and all we are thinking about is what WE are going to say next with no thought to what the other person is saying. I've done this much more than I'd like to admit. My archaeological nature to dig into the human psyche can ironically cause me to miss that which is sitting just on the surface of another person's experience. I'm so busy thinking about the next question that I want to ask, that I miss the response just given!

In relational conflict the ability to pay attention is essential. Instead of striving to get our own point across and prove that we are right, the situation can best be resolved by doing nothing but listening and paying attention to all aspects of the conversation. Sometimes being the watcher instead of the player can benefit all parties. As a wise friend told me,

> "I have learned that being an observer and not a participant of the game is the best option for my own heart and my own energy. But the observer does have power. The game may be played differently and experienced differently by the players just because someone is watching."
>
> —Gay Arner

For myself, I know that there are a few relationships in my life that have never really worked. I've always thought that if I would just keep working harder and digging deeper that all would eventually be made right. I don't know how many times I've thought that things had been fixed and I anticipated a fresh start, to have it all blow up in my face again. The blame game doesn't work here, either. Sometimes things just ARE! And sometimes it is best to let them be. That means I have to pay close attention and recognize when it is time to simply walk away.

Paying attention to myself is the next aspect of this resolution. I want to continue learning to listen to my own heart and more importantly come to fully trust what my heart is trying to tell me. Reflection of the past has shown me that my heart knows truth and CAN be trusted. It's my job now to really believe that.

At this point, some might ask why I didn't mention paying attention to God. For me, that is a given. If one is paying attention to things around them, the relationships they encounter and their own heart, then they ARE paying attention to God. Since mankind was banished from the Garden of Timeless Unity, for the most part, God speaks to us through things and people. And most importantly His Spirit dwells in our hearts if we invite Him in. Thus the commitment to pay attention will only enhance our relationship with God. And that brings us to the last part of our GPS . . .

Savor the Experience!

"For lack of attention, a thousand forms of loveliness elude us every day."

—Evelyn Underh

"What a wonderful life I've had. I only wish I had realized it sooner."

—French writer, Colette

Savor: To perceive with relish, to give oneself to the enjoyment of

I'm thinking that perhaps this bit of navigational advice is the best of the bunch. At least the most fun. And I certainly could use more of that in my life. From the definition of "savor, it would seem that in order to put the word into action, one must have an attitude deliberately turned towards the act–to perceive with relish. And that doesn't mean pass the ketchup and mustard! The word relish means to take pleasure in. In order to do that one must first be PRESENT.

"Leave the past to God's mercy. Leave the future to God's discretion. This moment is all there is."
(From "Spiritual Literacy" by Frederic and Mary Ann Brussat)

Being in the present connects intimately with paying attention. It takes practice. And that involves a certain kind of mental exercising. How often have I caught myself thinking about what's going to happen tomorrow, or how foolish I was yesterday? As children, we want to hurry and grow up, finish school, get rich and get married. And we want it to happen quickly. Then as we get older, we tend to look back over our life and wonder, "What if?" or "Why did that happen?"

While it is helpful to have goals for the future and learn from the past, I believe that much can be learned from dwelling in the now. Thinking of tomorrow can fill us with hope, excitement, fear or dread. Thinking of the past makes us feel sad, regretful, relieved and content. But being in the present is what brings us joy, pleasure, fun and a sense of awe and wonder!

Savoring the experience can be greatly enhanced by accepting Grace. For me, accepting Grace means allowing myself to believe the truth that I am beloved of God, just as I am. Because He is worthy and living in me, I am also worthy. I am set FREE when I truly understand what it means to rest in God's Grace! And this freedom brings true excitement, joy and awe! It is only when I 'm free from judging myself and others and free from expecting certain behaviors from all of us, that I can really savor life today!

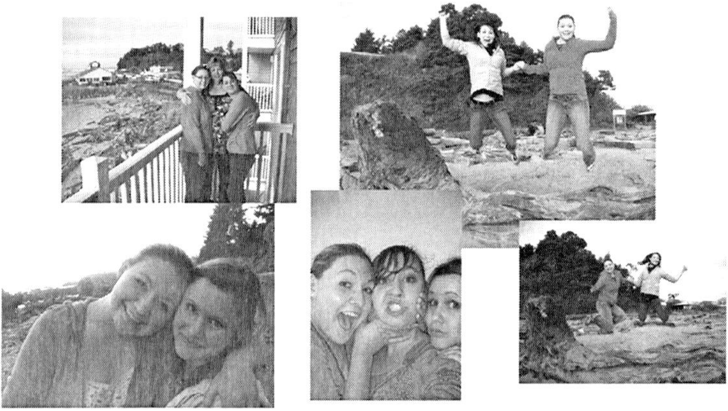

Myself and I

I've an empty nest and now find myself
with a stranger in my home.
She's lived with me all my life, but she's
no one I've ever really known.

She's been a tag-a-long and many
times, she's gotten in the way.
But I've usually just ignored her, not
given her the time of day.

Now she stands before me, willing to be a friend,
And I know that this relationship is one
that is important to amend.

At first it wasn't easy to look her in the eye,
But since it's pretty much just the two
of us, I've given it my best try.

I'm discovering we have things in common
and a few things I never knew,
I think she'll make a good companion
and be someone who is true.

Linda Harris

She definitely has her own opinions,
but she's easy to entertain.
She likes to ponder what it is that makes us
tick and loves to exercise her brain.

This could very well be the beginning
of something really great.
This friendship between myself and I,
let's simply call it fate.

—Linda

About the Author

Linda Harris currently resides in the Walla Walla Valley of Washington state. She is an elementary school teacher in a nearby Oregon public school. She is the proud mom of two beautiful daughters, Megan and Jessica.
Email: lindyharris729@yahoo.com

Published: 2015